# PRAISE FOR THE PLAYS OF ADAM RAPP

### STONE COLD DEAD SERIOUS

"Rapp . . . writes with an urgent, galloping imagination . . . *Stone Cold Dead Serious* . . . is the work of a playwright who is forging a real voice . . . Its rendering of the shared language of loved ones illustrates how families can remain intimate even when they are in shards. Its depiction of a working-class America that is unable to dream of anything beyond enduring is as sincerely sad a commentary on our culture as I've seen in recent memory. And its fear for young people is, unfortunately, deeply convincing."

—BRUCE WEBER, *The New York Times*

"Sharp and disquieting . . . Beneath the scurrilous comic banter and absurd surfaces is a mysterious recurrence of objects, actions, personae and language, in an oblique and haunting style reminiscent of Haruki Murakami's best fiction . . . *Stone Cold Dead Serious* works as a kind of venomous sustenance, dangerous but invigorating."

—ED PARK, *The Village Voice*

"A dark new American Gothic."

—*The New Yorker*

"A touching lesson about the importance of family and forgiveness."

—TERRY BYRNE, *Boston Herald*

"What an emotional landscape Rapp dramatizes! He is a poet of the down-and-out, of drugged human flotsam that, unbearable as it seems, gradually turns, under his intense gaze, into achingly recognizable human form. He is a poet of love among the abused, of the unbidden flower that forces its way up through the impenetrable concrete of circumstance . . . [*Stone Cold Dead Serious* is] intense, grimly lyrical and strangely sweet, a journey through a desperate world to emotional exhaustion and a fragile bud of hope."

—CHRISTOPHER RAWSON, *The Pittsburgh Post-Gazette*

"Both sociological study and surreal satire as the characters are whirled in and out of an absurd landscape. Rapp's deft ability at a Pinteresque, understated style of dialogue, inextricably linked to the timing of its delivery, pulls from this absurd family the kind of believable nuances necessary to keep the audience invested . . . Will leave your mind buzzing and your heart aching."

—BRANDON WOLCOTT, *Show Business Weekly*

"Powerfully written."

—ED SIEGEL, *The Boston Globe*

"[A] scabrous, poignant vision of suburban-American innocence lost."

—CAROLYN CLAY, *The Boston Phoenix*

## FASTER

"Spectacular end of the world weirdness [from] one of our favorite playwrights."

—*Time Out New York*

"Talented and highly prolific . . . Rapp . . . is brave and facile in his language, and he ventures [in *Faster*] where few writers are able or willing to go."

—BRUCE WEBER, *The New York Times*

"There's no want of energy [in] *Faster* . . . [Rapp] has a rising reputation for creating fast-talking, hard-hitting characters who make up in colorful language and an intensity of physical connection what they lack in, well, social graces."

—JEREMY GERARD, *New York*

"[Rapp] has made a name for himself writing about the darker things . . . *Faster* is no exception as it examines the complex relationship between hope and reality, faith and circumstance."

—RANEE JABER, *Show Business Weekly*

"The most anticipated and talked about play [at the 2002 Louisville Humana Festival]."

—*Back Stage*

"Adam Rapp [is] a busy and intelligent young writer . . . *Finer Noble Gases* . . . is a lament for society's lonely and alienated . . . Bright and funny."

—BRUCE WEBER, *The New York Times*

"Rapp boldly and honestly exposes a segment of society that most of us, thankfully, know only from a distance. [*Finer Noble Gases*] is a resounding warning about what happens when parents disconnect from their children and the young turn to drugs, television and other substances as emotional pacifiers."

—JUDITH EGERTON, *The Courier-Journal* (Louisville)

"The show everyone wanted to talk about . . . [*Finer Noble Gases*] taps into the ethos and ambience of . . . drugs, paranoia, and alienation."

—RICK PENDER, *Cincinnati CityBeat*

"The work of a promising writer."

—BILL FARK, *North County Times*

"Funny and shockingly obnoxious . . . [A] weird and frightening look at society's fringe elements . . . Rapp [is] ringing an alarm about the decline of humanity."

—JUDITH EGERTON, *The Louisville Scene*

STEVEN FREEMAN

# ADAM RAPP

## STONE COLD DEAD SERIOUS
### And Other Plays

*Adam Rapp* has been the recipient of the 1997 Herbert and Patricia Brodkin Scholarship; a fellowship to the Carmago Foundation in Cassis, France; two Lincoln Center LeComte du Nouy Awards; the 1999 Princess Grace Award for Playwriting; the 2000 Roger L. Stevens Award from the Kennedy Center Fund for New American Plays; a 2000 Suite Residency with Mabou Mines; and the 2001 Helen Merrill Award for Emerging Playwrights. He is the author of numerous plays, including *Nocturne* (Faber, 2002), which was awarded Boston's Elliot Norton Award for Best New Script as well as Best New Play by the Independent Reviewers of New England. It was chosen as one of the ten "Best Plays of 2000–2001" (the annual Chronicle of U.S. Theater) and was a finalist for the inaugural William Saroyan International Writing Prize. His plays have been produced at the Humana Festival of New American Plays, Victory Gardens in Chicago, the 24th Street Theatre in Los Angeles, the Juilliard School, the American Repertory Theatre in Cambridge, Massachusetts, Berkeley Repertory, New York Theatre Workshop, the Chashama and Rattlestick Theaters in New York, and the Bush Theatre in London. A graduate of Clark College in Dubuque, Iowa, he also completed the Lila Acheson Wallace Playwriting Fellowship at Juilliard. He is currently in post-production with his first film, *Winter Passing*.

Rapp is also the author of the novels *Missing the Piano, The Buffalo Tree, The Copper Elephant, Little Chicago, 33 Snowfish*, and the forthcoming *Under the Wolf, Under the Dog*. He lives in New York City.

ALSO BY ADAM RAPP

*Nocturne*

# STONE

# COLD

# DEAD

# SERIOUS

*And Other Plays*

■　▨　■　▪　▨

FABER AND FABER, INC.

*An affiliate of Farrar, Straus and Giroux*

NEW YORK

# STONE

# COLD

# DEAD

# SERIOUS

■ ▨ ■ ▨

*And Other Plays*

# ADAM RAPP

FABER AND FABER, INC.

An affiliate of Farrar, Straus and Giroux

18 West 18th Street, New York 10011

Distributed in Canada by Penguin Books of Canada Limited

Printed in the United States of America

FIRST EDITION, 2004

*Finer Noble Gases* was first published in 2002 in *Humana Festival 2002: The Complete Plays* by Smith and Kraus, Inc.

Lyrics from the song "Three Volcanoes" reprinted with permission of the author, Don Black.

Library of Congress Cataloging-in-Publication Data

Rapp, Adam.

  Stone cold dead serious and other plays / by Adam Rapp.— 1st ed.

     p.   cm.

  Contents: Stone cold dead serious—Faster—Finer noble gases.

  ISBN-13: 978-0-571-21139-5

  ISBN-10: 0-571-21139-9 (pb)

     1. East Village (New York, N.Y.)—Drama.   2. Swindlers and swindling—Drama.   3. Working class families—Drama.   4. Young adults—Drama.   5. Teenage boys—Drama.   6. Summer—Drama.   7. Devil—Drama.   I. Title.

PS3568.A6278S76 2004

812'.54—dc22

2003060352

*Designed by Gretchen Achilles*

www.fsgbooks.com

5   7   9   10   8   6

FOR  E. A. R.

*with love*

# CONTENTS

# ACKNOWLEDGMENTS

The author wishes to thank Darrell Larson, Michael Garcés, David Van Asselt and Louise Shannon of Rattlestick Theater, Amy Wegener, Tanya Palmer, and Marc Masterson of the Actors Theatre of Louisville, and especially Carolyn Cantor and David Korins of Edge Theater.

# STONE

# COLD

# DEAD

# SERIOUS

■ ▦ ■ ▦

*Stone Cold Dead Serious* was originally produced in Cambridge, Massachusetts, by the American Repertory Theater on February 6, 2002. It was directed by Marcus Stern; sets were designed by Christine Jones; costumes by Catherine Zuber; lights by John Ambrosone; and sound by David Remedios and Marcus Stern. The production stage manager was Jennifer Rae Moore. The cast was as follows:

| | |
|---|---|
| WYNNE LEDBETTER | *Matthew Stadelmann* |
| CLIFF LEDBETTER | *Guy Boyd* |
| SHAYLEE LEDBETTER/SHARICE | *Elizabeth Reaser* |
| LINDA LEDBETTER | *Deirdre O'Connell* |
| JACK GAM | *Robert Runck* |
| RANDALL "THE RANDYMAN" ROCKEYJOHN | *Philip Graeme* |

*Stone Cold Dead Serious* was subsequently produced in New York City by the Edge Theater Company at Chashama on March 28, 2003. It was directed by Carolyn Cantor; sets were designed by David Korins; costumes by Victoria Farrell; lights by Ben Stanton; and sound by Eric Shim. The production stage manager was Jeff Myers. The cast was as follows:

| | |
|---|---|
| WYNNE LEDBETTER | *Matthew Stadelmann* |
| CLIFF LEDBETTER/JACK GAM | *Guy Boyd* |
| SHAYLEE LEDBETTER/SHARICE | *Gretchen Cleevely* |
| LINDA LEDBETTER/SNAKE LADY | *Betsy Aidem* |
| RANDALL "THE RANDYMAN" ROCKEYJOHN | *Anthony Rapp* |

# CHARACTERS

WYNNE LEDBETTER                *sixteen, small for his age, a video game genius*

CLIFF LEDBETTER                *fiftyish, Wynne's father, an injured window glazer*

SHAYLEE LEDBETTER              *seventeen, Wynne's sister, a runaway*

LINDA LEDBETTER                *mid-forties, Wynne's mother, a waitress, exhausted*

JACK GAM                       *fiftyish, a salesman*

SHARICE                        *sixteen, Wynne's girlfriend, a fighter*

SNAKE LADY                     *mid-forties, an East Village eccentric*

RANDALL "THE RANDYMAN"
  ROCKEYJOHN                   *a hyperbolic Australian, a live-action death match pundit*

# SETTING

In and around the Chicago suburbs and New York City.

# ACT I

■  ▦  ■  ▦

## SCENE 1.

### THE LEDBETTERS

*The living room of a small house on the outskirts of Chicago,
somewhere near O'Hare Airport. Paneled walls. Drifts of coupons,
empty cans of Old Style. A color console TV that doubles as a coffee
table. Also on the coffee table is a block of shiny new knives. There is the
sense that nothing ever gets thoroughly cleaned. Upstage of the living
room a small kitchen visible through a cutout. Upstage left, a small
staircase leads to the second floor. Downstage right, the front door and a
window. The only light source other than the TV is the harsh kitchen
overhead spilling into the living room.*

*CLIFFORD LEDBETTER, fiftyish, heavy, unshaven, is beached on the
sofa, watching QVC. There are three or four pharmaceutical containers
on top of the coffee table. He is awake but appears to be in a state of
hypnotic sloth. Perhaps his mouth hangs open. Perhaps he drools. The
two men on the QVC are narrating sales pitches having to do with
baseball cards. CLIFF wears a housecoat, slippers, a white T-shirt. His
hair is ridiculous. He has been farting continuously and without shame.
Periodically, jets can be heard flying over the house.*

*In the kitchen the phone rings several times.*

CLIFF *continues staring at the TV, catatonic.*

WYNNE *enters through the front door, holding a paper sack. He bolts across the living room for the phone. In a blur we see that he is sixteen, small and thin. He wears corduroy pants, skater sneakers, and a rock-n-roll T-shirt. His hair is dyed blue.* CLIFF *continues staring at the soothing miracles of QVC.*

WYNNE (*from off*) Hello? . . . Hey . . . Yeah . . . Uh-huh . . . Hang on.

WYNNE *enters the living room, holding the phone, the cord stretching from the kitchen, still holding the paper sack.*

WYNNE Pop . . . Pop . . . *Pop* . . . (*covers the phone*) Hey, fuckhead! (*to phone*) He ain't responding . . . Yeah, he's up. I don't know . . . I'll try it. (*to* CLIFF) Cliff . . . Yo, Cliff . . . Clifford Ledbetter . . . CLIFFORD LEMOYNE LEDBETTER! (*to phone*) Didn't work . . . Yeah, he's been drinkin . . . I don't know . . . You want me to *hit* him? . . . Like *hit him* hit him? . . . *Where?* . . . Ma, I ain't gonna punch him in the balls . . . No way, he'll kill me, man . . . Okay, okay, fine, I'll do it . . .

WYNNE *puts the phone down, takes a step toward his dad, sets the paper sack on the TV, hesitates a moment, and then punches* CLIFF *in the balls.*

CLIFF Hey! You just punched me in the balls, man!
WYNNE Sorry, dude. Those were my instructions.
CLIFF From who?
WYNNE Ma.

CLIFF  Thanks a lot, Linda!

WYNNE  She's on the phone.

CLIFF  Wha?

WYNNE  The phone. She's on the phone.

CLIFF  Who's on the phone?

WYNNE  Ma. She wants to know if you want your potatoes baked or scalloped.

CLIFF  Where the fuck's the phone?

WYNNE  It's over there. Baked or scalloped?

CLIFF  Scalped.

WYNNE  And she wants to know on a scale of one to ten how your back is feelin. One bein the worst, ten bein the best.

CLIFF  Four-fifty for a Tiger Woods rookie card. Must be blue book value.

WYNNE  It's *two payments* of four-fifty.

CLIFF  Two payments?

WYNNE  Yeah, man—it's called the Flexplan. That's nine hundred bucks.

CLIFF  Well, I can't afford that.

WYNNE  Nobody can afford that. The Flexplan is fuckin larceny.

WYNNE *turns a lamp on.*

CLIFF  I went to school with a kid named Larceny. Larceny Dimitrovits. Drove a '64 Skylark. Hand-cleaned the engine every mornin in the parkin lot. Hood popped, shoulders hunched. Wiped her down with a warshcloth. Guy smelled like vinegar.

WYNNE  Pop.

CLIFF  I said scalped! Scalp the fuckers!

WYNNE *crosses to the kitchen.*

*Stone Cold Dead Serious*

CLIFF  Two payments of four-fifty. That ain't fair. I should write a letter and report those guys.

CLIFF *stands up very slowly, using every part of the sofa. He turns a full circle, disoriented.*

WYNNE  (*into phone*) He said he likes em scalped . . . Yeah, *scalped*—that's what he said . . . No he wouldn't give me a number . . . He's trashed again . . . I couldn't help it, Ma, he takes em when he takes em! I ain't a fuckin nurse! . . . All right, see ya in a few.

WYNNE *re-enters.*

WYNNE  Pop, sit back down . . . Sit down, Pop!

CLIFF *starts to cry.*

WYNNE  What's wrong?
CLIFF  I pooped again. It's goin all down my leg.
WYNNE  Jesus Christ, man.
CLIFF  I can't help it, it just starts comin out. Please don't tell Linda. If your ma finds out I pooped again she won't let me sleep in the bed with her.
WYNNE  Stay there.

WYNNE *exits to the kitchen, searches for* CLIFF's *diapers.*

WYNNE  What happened to your diapers?
CLIFF  I ran out.
WYNNE  You tell Ma?

ADAM RAPP

CLIFF  Yeah.

WYNNE  No you didn't. You gotta tell her, man.

WYNNE *re-enters with a wad of paper towels, hands them to* CLIFF.

CLIFF  Who're you, anyway?

WYNNE  Who *am* I?

CLIFF  I ain't never seen you before.

WYNNE  Dude, I'm your son.

CLIFF  My son don't got blue hair. His hair's black. Blackest hair I
ever seen. His name is Wynnewood. Wynnewood Jericho
Ledbetter. Who're you—Fuckhead Joe?

WYNNE  Pop, it's me, man—Wynne.

CLIFF  I wanna go to Cracker Barrel.

WYNNE  You ain't goin to Cracker Barrel.

WYNNE *exits to the bathroom, starts water in the tub.*

CLIFF  I wanna go to Cracker Barrel. Homemade Chicken-n-
Dumplings. Hickory Smoked Country Ham. Grilled Tenderloin.
Peach Cobbler with ice cream. Last year they had a punkin
carvin contest. Big huge fuckers. Punkins the size of Cadillac
Sevilles. They got em for sale under the old wilma tree. A million
inna half punkins. Carve up the jackalanner. Put a candle in it,
set her on the porch.

WYNNE  (*re-entering*) Pop, we don't got a porch.

CLIFF  Wha?

WYNNE  We-don't-got-a-porch-man. That was in Kankakee when
you were a kid. That tree's in Bourbonnais. You used to make us
get out of the car and run around it. You'd race us. We stopped
doin it after you sprained your ankle that time. Come on, Pop.

CLIFF  What ever happened to the wilma tree anyway?

WYNNE  Nothin happened to it. It's still there. I saw it last week when I went down to Carbondale with Palumbo. And it's will*ow,* tree. Let's go to the bathroom, okay?

*They exit to the bathroom.*

*The knob to the front door is jiggled. The failure of keys. Cursing from a young woman can be heard. Moments later* SHAYLEE *can be seen peering in through the living room window. The window is lifted, she quietly crawls through. She is seventeen, pretty but sickly-looking. She wears old jogging pants rolled down at the waist, old running shoes. She carries a bag that contains the few fragmented parts of her life. She looks around the living room, runs upstairs, comes back down. Perhaps she limps a bit. She studies the labels on the pill bottles. She opens the bottles, takes a few, chases with Old Style dregs. She stares at the block of knives, removes a small paring knife, puts it in her bag.*

*She crosses to the living room shelves and starts to rummage through stuff, looking for money, anything valuable, puts things in her bag.*

WYNNE *enters, watches her. After a moment,* SHAYLEE *turns, stands. They are frozen.*

SHAYLEE  Hey.

WYNNE  Hey.

SHAYLEE  What's up?

WYNNE  Nothin.

*He looks around to see what she's taken.*

SHAYLEE  What?

WYNNE  What?

SHAYLEE  So gimme a hug, ya little dick.

*He crosses to her. They hug. She goes for his pocket.*

SHAYLEE  Lend me five bucks.

WYNNE  No.

SHAYLEE  (*digging in*) Why not?

WYNNE  Cause I don't got it.

SHAYLEE  (*really digging in now*) Yes you do, Mr. Computer Fixer. Five fuckin bucks, man!

WYNNE *pushes her away. Some loose change falls out of his pocket.*
SHAYLEE *desperately goes after the scattered change.*

SHAYLEE  Smells like shit in here.

WYNNE  Where you been stayin?

SHAYLEE  At the Y.

WYNNE  What Y?

SHAYLEE  The one in Franklin Park.

WYNNE  Who's payin for it?

SHAYLEE  This guy Ed.

WYNNE  Ed who?

SHAYLEE  Just Ed. I met him near the candy machines.

WYNNE  Ma sees you here she'll call the cops.

SHAYLEE  So?

WYNNE  You're like shakin.

SHAYLEE  (*sitting*) No I ain't.

WYNNE  You look like shit.

SHAYLEE  You look like a geek.

WYNNE  You ain't eatin are you?

SHAYLEE  I eat.

WYNNE  You're so skinny.

SHAYLEE  I just ate somethin the other day.

WYNNE  What, you chewed an aspirin, drank some nose spray?

SHAYLEE  I ate a banana.

WYNNE *grabs the paper sack from under the coffee table.*

SHAYLEE  What's in the bag?

WYNNE  Nothin.

SHAYLEE  (*mocking*) Nothin.

WYNNE  It's a Taser gun.

*He takes it out, shows it to her.*

SHAYLEE  Where'd you get it?

WYNNE  From this guy Palumbo knows in Libertyville.

SHAYLEE  What's it for?

WYNNE  Tasering. Ever been Tasered?

SHAYLEE  No. Why, you wanna Taser me?

WYNNE  No. It's for protection.

SHAYLEE  How much was it?

WYNNE  I scored it for eighty bucks. They go for two hundred on the black market.

*He puts it in his back pocket.* SHAYLEE *pulls out a small box that contains many feeble cigarette butts, lights one, smokes.*

WYNNE  When'd you start smokin?

SHAYLEE  I don't know. At some point I guess. Where's Ma been hidin her cigarettes?

WYNNE  She quit.

SHAYLEE  Bullshit.

WYNNE  She did. Last month. She used the patch.

SHAYLEE  (*quickly rising, crossing to credenza behind the sofa, looting again*) Fuckin over-the-counter bitch.

WYNNE  Palumbo saw you in Joliet. He said you were on the casino boat and that you were with some rich Iranian dude who was wearin a popcorn bucket on his head.

SHAYLEE  His name's Amir and it's called a fez. He's Moroccan.

WYNNE  Palumbo said you were playin slots.

SHAYLEE  (*crossing back to the sofa, sitting, trying to smoke*) Amir was payin, I was pullin.

WYNNE  Palumbo said he tried talkin to you but you kept sayin you didn't know him and that your name was Katrina.

SHAYLEE  I guess I was Katrina that night.

WYNNE  He said you were dressed like a whore.

SHAYLEE  Little wop wouldn't know a whore if one walked up and spit on him.

WYNNE  He said you had so much makeup on you looked dead.

SHAYLEE  Maybe I am.

WYNNE  I love you, Shaylee.

SHAYLEE  Good. Gimme five bucks.

WYNNE  You should talk to Ma. Give her a call.

SHAYLEE  Fuck that bitch.

WYNNE  If you get your shit together she'd prolly let you come home.

SHAYLEE  I don't wanna get my shit together.

WYNNE  Pop misses you.

SHAYLEE  So?

WYNNE  He talks about you all the time. The other day he was in your closet holdin your nightgown.

SHAYLEE  Boo-hoo-hoo, what a fuckin drag, huh?

WYNNE  They kept your room just like it was. Your runnin trophies and everything.

SHAYLEE  Tell em to rent it out, board it up, have a fuckin garage sale.

*A beat.*

WYNNE  I'm goin to New York.

SHAYLEE  For what?

WYNNE  This video game competition. I'm one of the three finalists. If I win I get a shitloada money. I'll give you some. I could send it to you at the Y in Franklin Park. You could go to that place in Michigan and get clean. That place with all the maple trees.

SHAYLEE  Gimme five bucks I'll show you my pussy. (*pushing the front of her jogging pants down*) See?

WYNNE *steps away, crosses to the kitchen. After a silence:*

SHAYLEE  Drinkin alone, huh?

WYNNE  That's Pop.

SHAYLEE  Where is he?

WYNNE  In the tub.

SHAYLEE  What's he doin home?

WYNNE  He hurt his back.

SHAYLEE  Last time I was here I saw his dick. I was hidin in the shower. He walked in and took a piss. It looked like a mushroom. Like somethin that gets left in a salad bowl.

What happened to his back?

WYNNE  He herniated a disc.

SHAYLEE  Stupid fuck. How'd he do that?

WYNNE  Bendin over backwards glazin a window. He's sposed to have an operation to fuse his vertebrae but we can't afford it. He gets shooting pains down his legs. It fucks him up pretty bad. He shits his pants, has to wear diapers.

SHAYLEE  Is he gettin workmen's comp?

WYNNE  Yeah.

SHAYLEE  You know where he keeps his money?

WYNNE  Ma keeps it.

SHAYLEE  Where?

WYNNE  In her music box. But it's mostly checks.

SHAYLEE  (*starting for the stairs*) I can cash checks.

WYNNE  Don't take too many.

SHAYLEE  I'll take whatever I please.

WYNNE  Fine! Fuck it!


*She stops halfway up the stairs, sits.* WYNNE *fiddles with his Taser gun.*


SHAYLEE  Guess what?

WYNNE  What.

SHAYLEE  I got hepatitis. My armpits are yellow, wanna see?

WYNNE  No.

SHAYLEE  I fucked this Chink in the back of the 7-Eleven in Elk Grove. I think he gave it to me. His dick stunk like shit. I'm gonna buy a gun, hunt the fucker down. Stick it up his ass and pull the trigger . . . Got a girlfriend?

WYNNE  Sorta.

SHAYLEE  Who?

WYNNE  She's one of the three finalists.

SHAYLEE  What's her name?

WYNNE  Why?

SHAYLEE  Cause I'm jealous.

WYNNE  It's Sharice.

SHAYLEE  She a nigger?

WYNNE  I don't know.

SHAYLEE  Why not?

WYNNE  (*mumbling*) Cause I've never seen her.

SHAYLEE  What?

WYNNE  I've never seen her. I met her online. And so what if she was?

SHAYLEE  Niggers are dirty. Trust me, I know. Where's she from?

WYNNE  Crothersville, Indiana.

SHAYLEE  Small-town nigger, to boot.

WYNNE  If Ma heard you say nigger she'd fuckin die.

SHAYLEE  So.

WYNNE  So, you sound like one of those skinheads from Cicero.

SHAYLEE  I like those guys.

WYNNE  You're a racist.

SHAYLEE  No I ain't. I just don't like niggers.


*She descends the stairs, crosses to him on the sofa.*


SHAYLEE  Do you jerk off to her?

WYNNE  To who?

SHAYLEE  Shaniqua.

WYNNE  Sharice.

SHAYLEE  Sharice. You beat your meat to Sharice?

WYNNE  Sometimes.

*She administers a titanic titty twister.*

SHAYLEE  Cum on your stomach, think about tastin it?

WYNNE  (*wrenching away*) Fuck no! . . . What time is it, anyway?

SHAYLEE  Time to fuck and buy drugs. Why?

WYNNE  She's sposed to call.

SHAYLEE  Phone sex.

WYNNE  I'm in love with her, Shaylee.

SHAYLEE  Nigger phone sex.

WYNNE  We instant-message each other all the time. We're goin to New York together. I'm hitchin to Crothersville and then we're taking Greyhound the rest of the way.

SHAYLEE  Where the fuck is Crothersville?

WYNNE  Somewhere in the middle of the state, offa 65. She's mute.

SHAYLEE  How the fuck is she gonna call here if she's mute?

WYNNE  She's got this thing that she types into. Some sorta transmitter. An electronic voice speaks into the phone based on what she types.

SHAYLEE  (*getting off the sofa*) That's so fucked.

WYNNE  I think it's cool.

SHAYLEE *crosses to the kitchen.*

SHAYLEE  What if the voice is all macho or somethin?

WYNNE  I don't care.

SHAYLEE  What if she sounds like a cop?

WYNNE  I really don't care. I think I'm in love.

SHAYLEE  (*from the kitchen*) You better fuck her before you start talkin about love, Wynne.

WYNNE  Why?

SHAYLEE  (*re-entering with a bottle of vodka*) Cause her pussy might be dry.

SHAYLEE *crosses to the sofa, sits.* WYNNE *follows her.*

WYNNE  I ain't in love with her pussy.

SHAYLEE  What are you in love with, her e-mail address?

WYNNE  I don't know, Shaylee. I don't have the slightest idea what she looks like and I'm totally in love with her. And tell me this isn't weird: You know how my e-mail address is dog on mars at mindspring dot com? Well, hers is dog on venus at mindspring dot com. Pretty fuckin trippy, huh?

SHAYLEE  Romeo and Juliet.

WYNNE  (*sitting on the sofa*) Mars and Venus, man.

SHAYLEE  Romeoville and Joliet.

SHAYLEE *takes a slug of vodka, almost retches.*

SHAYLEE  So you're still playin that video game, huh?

WYNNE  Yeah. I solved it. That's why I'm a finalist.

SHAYLEE  Fuckin genius.

WYNNE  There's only three of us. They're gonna film the championship. Put it on cable.

SHAYLEE  Wynne the boy genius.

WYNNE  I ain't a boy.

SHAYLEE  If I cracked your head open I bet your brain would be huge.

WYNNE  If I win I'm gonna send you some money, Shaylee. You can go to that place in Michigan with the maple trees.

SHAYLEE  Fuck the maple trees.

WYNNE  You're gonna die if you don't get help.

SHAYLEE  I met this guy at a truck stop. His name was Jesus. He looked like Art Garfunkle if Art Garfunkle was a spic. He told me my soul was floatin around somewhere in the stratosphere. He kept callin me a floater. I fucked him in Centralia while I was on my period and I had to go to this clinic cause I forgot to take my tampon out. This doctor had to remove it with salad tongs. Fuckin place was full of refugees and derelicts.

WYNNE  You can take whatever you want outta my room.

SHAYLEE  What would I take?

WYNNE  Take my Playstation 2. You could prolly get fifty bucks for it.

SHAYLEE  You don't want your fuckin Playstation?

WYNNE  It's too easy.

*She smokes.*

SHAYLEE  This chick I met at the Y told me you can kill yourself by slashin your wrists in the bathtub. She said it don't hurt if you make the water warm enough cause it tricks your brain.

CLIFF  (*from off*) Hey!

*They both sit up.*

WYNNE  You better go.

SHAYLEE  You ain't gonna give me five bucks?

*He goes in his pocket, produces two. She snatches the cash.*

SHAYLEE  I'll suck your dick for two more.

CLIFF  (*from off*) Hey, fuckhead!

WYNNE  You really gonna buy a gun?

SHAYLEE  (*mocking*) You really gonna buy a gun?

CLIFF  (*from off*) Hey, Fuckhead Joe, is somethin burnin? Smells like the house is on fire!

WYNNE *takes* SHAYLEE's *cigarette, drops it in a beer can, starts to cross to the bathroom with* CLIFF's *pajamas.*

WYNNE  (*turning back*) Ma's music box is in her closet under Grandma Ruth's Christmas Eve quilt.

SHAYLEE *kisses him hard on the mouth, exits quickly up the stairs.* WYNNE *exits.*

*Moments later,* WYNNE *rushes back out, runs up the stairs, looks down the hall. The phone starts to ring in the kitchen.* WYNNE *runs for the phone.* CLIFF *enters from the bathroom. They meet head-on at the threshold of the kitchen.* WYNNE *is trapped between* CLIFF *and the wall. The phone continues ringing.* WYNNE *breaks free, lurches for the phone, answers it.*

WYNNE  Hello? . . . (*slamming the phone down*) Motherfucker!

CLIFF  Wha?

WYNNE  I missed my phone call!

CLIFF  What phone call? You don't get phone calls.

WYNNE  Fuck off, man, I do, too.

CLIFF  Who would call *you*?

WYNNE  Forget it. Back to the sofa.

CLIFF  I don't wanna go back to the sofa, I wanna go to Cracker Barrel.

WYNNE *pulls the Taser gun on* CLIFF.

WYNNE  Pop, get back to the sofa before I Taser your fat ass!

CLIFF  Where'dja get that?

WYNNE  Don't worry about where I got it, I got it.

CLIFF  I seen one of them on QVC.

WYNNE  Well now there's one pointed directly at your grille. Back to the couch, man. Now!

CLIFF  Okay, fine. Jeez!

*They make their way back to the sofa, the Taser gun trained on* CLIFF. CLIFF *sits.* WYNNE *puts the Taser gun back in his pocket, sits next to him. Only the sound of QVC.* CLIFF *farts rather explosively.* WYNNE *crosses to the chair.*

CLIFF  Who was here?

WYNNE  What?

CLIFF  Someone was here . . . Shaylee. Was Shaylee here?

WYNNE  No, why?

CLIFF  I can smell her. Same smell she had as a baby. Like holdin your hand real close to your face. Holdin it real close like so. (*he holds his hand real close to his face, smells*) She was such a pretty baby. She squeaked. You sure she wasn't here?

WYNNE  No one was here, Pop.

CLIFF  She was so little. You could hold her right there in your hand. Talk to her like she understood stuff.

WYNNE  Here, take a pill.

*He gives* CLIFF *a pill.* CLIFF *swallows it dry.*

CLIFF  Hey, how old are you, anyway?

WYNNE  How *old* am I?

CLIFF  What are you now, seventeen, eighteen?

WYNNE  I'm fuckin sixteen, man.

CLIFF  When I was sixteen I worked.

WYNNE  I work.

CLIFF  You do?

WYNNE  I fix computers, remember?

CLIFF  Huh.

WYNNE  That's your last bottle of painkillers, man. This shit is
fryin your brain.

CLIFF  When I was sixteen I joined a band of glaziers.

WYNNE  I know. There were hundreds of you and you'd follow
tornadoes around on a tour bus.

CLIFF  That's right. We'd follow the tomatoes around.

WYNNE  Tornadoes.

CLIFF  We'd fix all the greenhouses. I used to read the weather
maps. Look for the tomatoes. Few years later I met that guy
from the movies.

WYNNE  Sir Lawrence Olivier. I know, Pop.

CLIFF  At the University of Indiana at Bloomington. In
Bloomington, Indiana. Guy was sittin right there at the bus stop.
I said, "Hey, Hamlet!" He gave me his autograph and then he got
on the bus. Just like that. What a guy.

*They watch the TV for a moment.*

CLIFF  My fuckin nuts hurt.

WYNNE  That's cause I punched you in the balls.

CLIFF  You did?

WYNNE  Yeah, man. I broke your big ass down.

CLIFF  Huh.

*The sound of a car parking, car door opening and closing.*

CLIFF  Hey, where'd that cat go?

WYNNE  What cat?

CLIFF  That little cat we had.

WYNNE  Pop, we never had a cat.

CLIFF  Sure we did. Little fucker'd walk around, stare at you.

WYNNE  That was my guinea pig, man. It's dead. Shaylee kept feedin it Dexatrim. Fuckin thing starved to death.

CLIFF  I swear we had a cat.

LINDA *enters carrying a tin of lasagna, a tin of scalloped potatoes, and a large sack of groceries. She is in her mid-forties. She is wearing a waitress uniform and has a smoker's voice. She sets her armload on the TV.*

CLIFF  Hey Linda, didn't we have a cat?

LINDA  We had a guinea pig. Shaylee starved it to death with those diet pills.

CLIFF  What she name it?

WYNNE  His name was Jack. But everyone called it Cokehead.

CLIFF  Cokehead! Here kitty-kitty!

WYNNE  (*carrying groceries to the kitchen*) It was a fuckin guinea pig, man!

LINDA  What was that awful name she tried givin it at first?

WYNNE  (*popping his head out of the kitchen*) Dickburn.

LINDA  Yeah, *Dickburn.* (*kissing* CLIFF *on the crown of his head*) How awful is that? Not in my house.

*Stone Cold Dead Serious*                                        25

WYNNE His name was Jack.

CLIFF Jack Cokehead. Best goddamn cat I ever seen.

LINDA Hey, who was smokin in here?

WYNNE Nobody.


WYNNE *enters the kitchen.*


LINDA Someone was here and they were smokin.

CLIFF Smells like the fuckin house was on fire.

LINDA Wynne, was your sister here?

WYNNE I don't know.

LINDA Well, you've been home ain't it?

WYNNE Yeah, but I wasn't guardin the fuckin door.

LINDA Well, what the heck were you doin all day?

WYNNE I was down here with Pop.

CLIFF He left me alone. I almost died.

WYNNE Bullshit I left you alone. I was upstairs in my room.

CLIFF He went out. Left me alone to die.

LINDA Did you go out of the house, Wynne?

WYNNE What?

LINDA You heard me, smart guy.

WYNNE Yeah, but just for little while.

LINDA I thought I asked you not to leave.

WYNNE It was only for an hour.

LINDA You know what your sister's capable of.

WYNNE I needed some fresh air. It smells like farts in here.

LINDA Wynne, if you say you're gonna stay, then I'd appreciate
you stickin to your word. You know your father's condition.
The pills make him sleepy. If I knew you were gonna go out
I woulda called Marna and had her come over. For all we

know, your sister's upstairs right now robbin us
blind.

LINDA *starts for the stairs.*

WYNNE (*running to the stairs, cutting her off*) SO I'LL CALL
NEXT TIME! I'M FUCKIN SORRY, OKAY?!
LINDA  Was he smokin, Cliff? Wynne, were you smokin? Don't
you lie to me.
WYNNE  I wasn't.
LINDA  Let me smell your breath.
WYNNE  Back off, Geraldo.
LINDA  Your father wasn't smokin, was he? Cliff, you better notta
been smokin. It took me two months to get off the Merits. I
spent half my tip money on patches. You know I start cravin
cigarettes if I'm around em. (*to* WYNNE) Look at this house. It's a
dang pigsty. Wynne, help me clean up.

WYNNE *starts to gather beer cans.* LINDA *retrieves the food from the TV,
crosses to kitchen. Halfway there she drops the lasagna. It spills on the floor.*

LINDA  Oh, crymie! That lasagna cost me seven dollars! Cliff,
stop diggin in your nose.

LINDA *goes into the kitchen, comes back with a rag, starts scooping the
lasagna back into its tin.*

LINDA  Who put the air conditioner on the kitchen table?
WYNNE  I did.
LINDA  What the heck for?

WYNNE  I was tryin to fix it.

LINDA  What's wrong with it?

WYNNE  I don't know, it stopped workin.

LINDA  Whattaya mean it stopped workin, it's a dang Maytag. Maybe it needs Freon. A lot of em need Freon.

WYNNE  It ain't the Freon.

LINDA  How do you know?

WYNNE  Cause I checked.

LINDA  That thing ain't even a year old. I got it at Kresge's just last summer.

WYNNE  The thing that holds the fan belt's all fucked up. I called customer service and they said it would cost more to fix it than it would to buy a new one.

LINDA  But it's under warranty.

WYNNE  No it ain't.

LINDA  It is too.

WYNNE  Ma, you didn't get the warranty.

LINDA  I did so.

WYNNE  No you didn't, Ma. I was with you when you bought the thing. It was an extra twenty bucks and you didn't wanna pay it.

LINDA  I shoulda went to Service Merchandise and got mine when Donna got hers. I ain't goin to Kresge's no more.

*She cleans.* CLIFF *farts rather explosively.*

LINDA  Excuse you.

CLIFF  Ha.

LINDA  You're the Ha. (*to* WYNNE) Did that guy from the bank call again? Mr. Worrell?

WYNNE  Yeah.

LINDA  What'd he say?

WYNNE  He said what he always says. We're late on the mortgage, when are we gonna pay, this can't keep happenin. Same old shit.

LINDA  He's actually a really nice man. I saw him at the restaurant with his family. They got a little girl and she's so cute.

WYNNE  He's a fuckin vulture, Ma!

LINDA  (cleaning) He's just doin his job. That ain't no easy job, Wynne, houndin folks for their mortgages.

WYNNE  How short are we?

LINDA  We're short.

WYNNE  How short?

LINDA  Four hundred dollars. If your father didn't buy those dang knives we'd be okay this month.

CLIFF  Cutco Cutlery. Best knives in the world.

LINDA  Nothin like a little QVC to ruin your summer. If you see your father with my bankcard again you take it away from him.


WYNNE *reaches into his pocket, removes a knot of money, hands it to* LINDA.


LINDA  Where'd you get that?

WYNNE  I've had it.

LINDA  You've had it from what?

WYNNE  I fixed that guy's hard drive.

LINDA  What guy?

WYNNE  That guy who I met at the restaurant. The guy from Rosemont.

LINDA  Alvin?

WYNNE  Yeah, Alvin. The rich guy with the hair.

CLIFF  Alvin and the Chipmunks.

*Stone Cold Dead Serious*

LINDA That guy's a little weird, Wynne. He's always tryin to get one of the chefs to go for a ride in his Lexus with him. Sally thinks he's a homo.

WYNNE He ain't a homo.

LINDA How do you know?

WYNNE Cause he's married.

LINDA He's too good-lookin to not be a homo, Wynne. And besides, what does he do anyway?

WYNNE He works at the stock exchange. He's got a seat on the floor. You're the one who introduced me to him.

CLIFF He's a homo!

WYNNE Pop, you don't even know the dude!

CLIFF Everyone's a homo! I'm a fuckin homo!

LINDA You didn't go in his Lexus with him, did you?

WYNNE I told you I fixed his hard drive. It wouldn't spin down right, I fixed it.

LINDA You're tryin to tell me he gave you four hundred bucks for fixin his computer?

WYNNE Just take the money, Ma.

*She takes it, folds it into her bra. She starts to cry.*

WYNNE Ma.

*She tries to stop.*

WYNNE Don't cry, Ma.

LINDA I did a dang double today. Eighty-four lousy bucks on a double. Fat-ass Glenn's yellin at all the gals. "Stop socializin! Bus your goddamn tables!"

WYNNE That guy's such a dick.

LINDA Sweatin all over the food! Fat-ass Glenn! (*wiping her face*) I'm sorry. I shouldn't get like this in fronta you.
WYNNE It's okay, Ma. Here, take some more.

*He produces some more money. She takes it.*

LINDA Thanks, honey.

LINDA *rises, kisses* WYNNE, *crosses to the kitchen.*

LINDA Now ask your father what he wants to drink. I got bug juice and chocolate milk . . . It's so dang hot in here.
WYNNE Pop, you want bug juice or chocolate milk?
CLIFF Old Style.
WYNNE We're outta Old Style.
CLIFF Eight ninety-five a case at the Day-n-Night.
WYNNE I ain't goin to the fuckin Day-n-Night.
CLIFF Eight ninety-five a case. Milwaukee's Best for seven in a quarter.

LINDA *brings the tin of scalloped potatoes and three paper plates out to the top of the TV. She exits and returns with a thin roll of paper towels, three forks, a serving utensil, sets stuff down, exits again, returns with three glasses and a gallon of bug juice.* LINDA *pours bug juice into each glass.*

WYNNE *scoops potatoes onto each plate, hands a plate and glass of bug juice to* CLIFF, *grabs his own plate, sits on the sofa between his parents.*

LINDA I got chocolate milk in the fridge, too.

*Stone Cold Dead Serious*

CLIFF *claps twice so that the lamp next to the sofa turns on. They all begin eating. After a silence:*

LINDA  I think we should start goin to church again.
WYNNE  Why?
LINDA  Whattaya mean *why*. Does there gotta be a *why*?
WYNNE  Yeah.
LINDA  Well, for one thing, we're sposed to be Catholic and your Grandma Ruth's been gettin on my case about that. We have certain responsibilities.

And Marna's been collectin these portraits of the saints. She's been bringin em into work to show the gals. They're the most beautiful things. There's this one of St. Christopher and he's carryin the Baby Jesus across this stream on his shoulders.

What a handsome guy that St. Christopher was. By the way, what happened to that picture of St. Anthony of Padua we had hangin over the kitchen table? The one where he's sittin in the gazebo holdin a sea bass?
CLIFF  They got chicken gumbo at Cracker Barrel. Best gumbo around.
LINDA  Gazebo, do-do brain. Not gumbo. (*to* WYNNE) Marna was tellin me the most interestin things about St. Anthony of Padua. Did you know he lived in a cave in Italy and that he spoke in multiple tongues and that legend says he was such a good public speaker that even the fish would listen? That's prolly why he's holdin that sea bass. Cliff, get your dang hand outta your pants!
CLIFF  Fuckhead Joe punched me in the nuts.
LINDA  Oh, ha your nuts. I wonder what the heck happened to that picture. I wanted to show it to Marna.
WYNNE  Ma, what's with the sudden religious trip? We don't even say Grace, man.

ADAM RAPP

LINDA  I know, but we used to.

WYNNE  We did?

LINDA  Sure we did, ain't it, Cliff?

CLIFF  Wha?

LINDA  You were too little to remember, Wynne. Shaylee would say it. Bless us O lord, for these Thy gifts—

CLIFF  (*lucid*) Which we are about to receive, from Thy bounty, through Christ our Lord, Amen.

SHAYLEE *appears on the staircase, watches them.*

LINDA  See? We said Grace.

WYNNE  Did he just pray? Pop, did you just fuckin pray?

CLIFF  Wha?

LINDA  We could start goin to church again. Whattaya say, Cliff, I think it would be good for us. Lainy the new cashier says there's this really nice parish in Aurora. Our Lady of Good Councel. She says they're real welcome to new folks comin in.

WYNNE  Church is for cowards.

LINDA  No it ain't. Why do you say that?

WYNNE  Buncha guilty people actin like wimps about it.

LINDA  Wynne!

WYNNE  God don't give a fuck. He's an asshole, man.

LINDA  No he ain't.

WYNNE  He's an asshole and people go to church cause they're fuckin scared of him.

LINDA  No they don't either.

WYNNE  Why do they go, then?

LINDA  Well, some go to pray. Some go just to think or take communion and get rid of their sins. I personally like singin the hymns and stuff.

WYNNE  What a waste.

LINDA  It ain't a waste! Wynne, when you were a little boy you used to pray!

WYNNE  That's only cause I wanted toys.

LINDA  That don't matter. You still prayed.

WYNNE  Well, *you* can start goin to church again, but I ain't.

LINDA  Why not?

WYNNE  Cause I'm leavin.

LINDA  You're leavin?

WYNNE  Yep.

LINDA  You're leavin for where?

WYNNE  Ma, I got an announcement to make.

LINDA  You do?

WYNNE *rises off the sofa, stands.*

WYNNE  Yeah, man. So pay attention

LINDA  Okay.

WYNNE  Pop, you listenin?

CLIFF  Wha?

WYNNE  Stop eatin—I'm makin an announcement.

CLIFF  Okay.

CLIFF *stops eating. They stare at* WYNNE.

WYNNE  I'm goin to New York City.

CLIFF  Ha.

WYNNE  I am, you fuckin sloth!

LINDA  Wynne, you can't go there.

WYNNE  Yes I can, Ma.

CLIFF  New York City—ha.

WYNNE  You know that video game I been playin for the past six months—*Tang Dynasty*?

LINDA  Yeah.

WYNNE  Well I solved the fucker and there's a *Tang Dynasty* Superchampionship in New York City and I'm a finalist. There's only three of us. Only three people in the whole goddamn country solved it.

LINDA  Well, congratulations, honey, but you can't go there.

WYNNE  I'm one of the three they invited, Ma, and I'm goin. My shit's packed and I'm leavin tonight.

LINDA  Whattaya mean you're leavin tonight? You can't leave tonight!

WYNNE  Watch me.

LINDA  And how are you plannin on gettin there exactly?

WYNNE  I'm gettin a ride to Crothersville, Indiana.

LINDA  You're gettin a ride from who?

WYNNE  Palumbo's droppin me off where 65 connects with 80/94 and I'm hitchhikin.

LINDA  You can't hitchhike, Wynne! Hitchhikin's so dangerous anymore. It's like suicide.

WYNNE  I can protect myself.

LINDA  Oh yeah, how?

CLIFF  He's got a Taser gun.

LINDA  You got a Taser gun!

CLIFF  Got it off QVC.

WYNNE  I did not get it off QVC. That's your trip, man.

CLIFF  Sat right here and watched him. Called em up and everything. Fuckhead Joe.

WYNNE  You're the fuckhead, Pop.

LINDA  Wynne, if you used my credit card to buy a dang Taser—

WYNNE  Ma, I got it from this guy Palumbo knows! He sells em down in Carbondale. Pop's talkin outta his ass again.

LINDA  Well, what the heck's in Indiana?

WYNNE  That's where I'm hookin up with one of the other finalists. I'm spendin the night and in the morning we're taking Greyhound the rest of the way east. The finals are gonna be broadcast on TV.

CLIFF  TV, huh?

WYNNE  Yeah, man. T-motherfuckin-V. You guys can sit here right on the sofa and watch me win.

LINDA  What do you win?

WYNNE  Money.

LINDA  How much money?

WYNNE  A shitload. Winner gets a million bucks.

LINDA  I don't believe you.

WYNNE  I got the contract upstairs in my room. I can go get it if you want.

CLIFF  I knew a guy who won a million bucks once. He bought condos down in Florida. Turned out to be swampland. Nothin but alligators and toilet water.

WYNNE  If I win I'm gonna use the money to help Pop get that operation and pay off the rest of the mortgage.

LINDA  Well, that's thoughtful.

WYNNE  Maybe start my own business fixin computers. Incorporate and everything. Ma, you could like do my books and shit.

LINDA  I like bookkeepin. Sometimes I help out at the restaurant when Glen's busy with stuff.

WYNNE  I was gonna maybe give some to Shaylee, too. Help her get clean.

LINDA  Well that's a laugh.

WYNNE  Why is that a laugh?

LINDA  Cause, honey, one has to *wanna* get clean. Shaylee don't wanna get clean.

WYNNE  She might, though. If I came back with some money she might wanna get clean.

CLIFF  Shaylee was the cleanest kid I ever knew. Cleaner than Christmas, that kid.

WYNNE  Well, anyway, that's what I'm doin. And I'm leavin tonight, as soon as we're finished eatin.

SHAYLEE *goes back upstairs. They eat to QVC.*

CLIFF  Potatoes are fuckin good, Lin.

CLIFF *farts like a French horn.* WYNNE *scoots toward* LINDA. *She hugs him close.*

LINDA  I don't think I can let you go, Wynne.

WYNNE  I'm goin.

CLIFF  Let him go, Linda. Let the kid go.

LINDA  Thinkin about you on that highway.

WYNNE  I'll only be gone a few days.

LINDA  But who's gonna help your father?

WYNNE  Call Marna.

CLIFF  Yeah, call Marna. I like Marna.

LINDA  I guess I could call Marna.

CLIFF  Marna takes me to Cracker Barrel.

LINDA  Well, what exactly happens at these finals?

WYNNE *rises off the sofa again, excited.*

*Stone Cold Dead Serious*

WYNNE  Three of us go to this unnamed site in the East Village and we have it out.

LINDA  What's the East Village?

WYNNE  It's in New York. It's like a neighborhood.

LINDA  Whattaya mean you have it out?!

WYNNE  I mean we compete, man. Except, insteada playin the video game it like comes to life. The three *Tang Dynasty* Broadswordsmen actually enter and we go hand-to-hand.

LINDA  Three *Tang Dynasty* Broadswordsmen enter where exactly?

WYNNE  An armored room in an undisclosed location in the East Village, that's all we know. Whoever kills the Broadswordsman with the golden sun on his chest wins the million and gets a blue star tattooed to his head.

LINDA  You're fighting guys with swords?!

WYNNE  Yeah, and they're like these totally ripped expert mercenaries, too.

LINDA  Well, that's not fair! Cliff, does that sound fair to you?

CLIFF  I say shoot the fuckers! Taser their macaroni asses!

WYNNE  *Mercenaries*, man!

LINDA  How do they expect you to defend yourself?

WYNNE  They give us each a wakizashi. So it's totally fair.

LINDA  What the heck's a wakizashi?

WYNNE  It's a sword. The blade's like a foot and a half long.

CLIFF  Kawasaki makes a good motorcycle, Lin.

LINDA  He's talkin about a sword, Cliff! A goddang sword!

WYNNE  And we get one optional weapon of choice. That's how come I got the Taser gun. So I'll have the wakizashi and the Taser.

CLIFF  Why don't you take a machine gun? Pack some fuckin heat, man!

ADAM RAPP

WYNNE  No firearms allowed. Stun guns, Tasers, and pepper spray were our three options.

LINDA  Crymie, Wynne, you can't participate in somethin like that! It don't even sound legal!

WYNNE  Ma, it's totally legal. I signed a waiver sayin I was responsible for my own life and everything. It was part of the contract.

LINDA  Wynne, this is such a nightmare. Cliff, ain't this a nightmare?

CLIFF  I think it's pretty fuckin cool.

WYNNE  Ma, I've been trainin for this for the past six months. Check out my abs, man.

*He pulls his shirt up, revealing his abs.*

WYNNE  Punch me.

LINDA  Oh, crymie.

WYNNE  Come on, Ma, punch me.

LINDA *taps his stomach.*

WYNNE  Harder.

*She taps his abs harder.* WYNNE *quickly crosses to* CLIFF.

WYNNE  Come on, Pop. It's time to render me inoperable. Blaze a hole in my abs.

CLIFF *tries to punch* WYNNE, *but* WYNNE *evades it swiftly, mock attacking him, then patting him on the back.*

WYNNE  See? Me and Palumbo have been goin to Zion every Sunday to play paintball and this Japanese dude from Norridge has been teachin me kendo.

LINDA  What Japanese dude from Norridge?

WYNNE  His name is Slice. He's a total badass. He trained me on the wakizashi. I'm a fierce and brutal weapon of death.

LINDA  You are not a fierce and brutal weapon of death, Wynne, you're a dang boy!

WYNNE  Ma, the other day I cut a pineapple in half while it was in the air. A pineapple and a Maxwell House coffee can.

LINDA  Who the heck's this kendo?

WYNNE  Kendo ain't nobody. Kendo's the Way of the Sword, man. Slice taught me all about it. How to conquer my ego and keep my mushin up. The way of the Samurai.

LINDA  The way of the who?

WYNNE  When a cow drinks water it becomes milk. When a snake drinks water it becomes poison.

LINDA  What the heck are you talkin about?!

WYNNE  The way of the Samurai is a natural way of the Universe, Ma, and to learn it, one must live one's life from first to last in self-control. I know all about that stuff now.

LINDA  I want the phone number of this Slice fella. Someone needs to talk to his parents.

CLIFF  I played Keno in Nevada once. Nevada, Las Vegas.

LINDA  (lunging at WYNNE, clinging to him) You can't go, Wynne! I ain't lettin you go!

WYNNE  Ma . . . Ma . . . Let go, Ma!


WYNNE pries himself loose. LINDA goes after him. WYNNE pulls out the Taser gun.

WYNNE  Back off, Ma, or I'll Taser your ass!

LINDA  (*freezing*) Do somethin, Cliff!

CLIFF  Do what?

LINDA  I don't know! Talk to him! He's your son, too!

CLIFF  That ain't my son. My son's hair ain't blue, it's black.
That's Fuckhead Joe . . . Lin, you're blockin the TV.

LINDA *moves.*

WYNNE  Wish me luck, Ma.

LINDA  Good luck, Wynne.

WYNNE  Wish me luck, Pop.

CLIFF  Ha!

WYNNE  Sunday night, Channel Thirty-seven. I'm comin home
with a blue star tattooed on my head, okay?

LINDA  Okay.

WYNNE  Stop cryin.

*She tries to stop crying.*

WYNNE  Make sure to give that cash to that dude from the bank.

LINDA  Okay.

WYNNE  And don't worry about the air conditioner. I'll take care
of it when I get back. In fact, throw the fuckin thing out. After I
win, we're gettin central air.

LINDA *nods.*

WYNNE  Man, you gotta stop cryin. I ain't leavin like this . . . Pop,
you got potatoes all over your face.

CLIFF *wipes his face.*

WYNNE  And Ma, make sure to get him a new thinga diapers.
LINDA  I'm goin to K mart tomorrow.
WYNNE  One finds life through conquering the fear of death
within one's heart. You gotta empty the mind of all forms of
attachment, make a balls-out, go-for-broke charge at your
opponent, and destroy him with a single, decisive slash. Togo
Shigekata said that. Or somethin like that. I love you guys.

WYNNE *lowers the Taser gun, exits.*

LINDA *crosses to the door, stares out, crosses back to the sofa, begins to
clean. Lights fade.*

ADAM RAPP

# SCENE 2.

## LATER THAT NIGHT.
## A NEW YORKER.

*The Interior of a Chrysler New Yorker. A* MAN, *fiftyish, is driving, the light from the dash glowing on his face. He wears a white shirt and an expensive tie. He is clean-shaven and well-kempt.* WYNNE *is sitting in the passenger seat, holding his gym bag. It is raining.*

MAN  So where you goin again?

WYNNE  Crothersville.

MAN  Crothersville, huh? What's in Crothersville?

WYNNE  Um. A friend.

MAN  Well, we could all use a friend, now and then, God knows that. (*pause*) You from around here?

WYNNE  I'm from Chicago.

MAN  That's what I thought. I seen you over there on the shoulder and I says to myself I says I'll bet two paychecks and a box of Chiclets that this poor fella's from the Windy City. Chicago, Illinois—now there's a town. You got the Sears Tower. The Lake. Navy Pier and all that . . . So why are you hitchhikin, you broke?

WYNNE  I got money.

*Stone Cold Dead Serious*                                                43

MAN  A solvent hitchhiker. Interesting.

WYNNE  I just felt it was somethin I needed to do.

MAN  I can understand that. The need to do a thing.

WYNNE  I'm sorta on this journey.

MAN  Aren't we all, aren't we all.

*A silence.*

WYNNE  Um. You got a radio in this thing?

MAN  The Chrysler New Yorker? Are you kidding me, stranger?

*The* MAN *turns on the radio to some Chuck Mangione. They listen for a moment.* WYNNE *turns the dial, finds some Wu Tang Clan or something like that. After a moment, the* MAN *turns the radio off altogether. A silence.*

MAN  Wanna smoke a joint?

WYNNE  Um, you're like drivin, dude.

MAN  Oh, I'm used to it. Helps relax me. Stressful job.

*A pause.*

MAN  Aren't you gonna ask me what my job is?

WYNNE  Um. What's your job?

MAN  Well, I sell cutlery, actually.

WYNNE  Like knives?

MAN  That's right. I drive around with a trunk fulla knives. But it's not just knives. It's all sortsa stuff. What's your name?

WYNNE  Um, Danny.

MAN  Hi, Danny. I'm Jack. Jack W. Gam, Junior.

JACK *extends his hand.* WYNNE *regards it, shakes.*

JACK  Nice to meet you, Danny.
WYNNE  Watch out!

*They swerve.*

WYNNE  Jesus, man! Holy shit that was close! You want me to drive?!
JACK  Oh, that won't be necessary.
WYNNE  Dude, that was a fucking semi!

*A pause.*

JACK  As I was saying: It's not just knives, Danny. It's utility shears, serving implements, barbecuing utensils. Cutco Cutlery encompasses a vast and versatile strata.
WYNNE  You sell *Cutco*?

*From some unknown region,* JACK *produces a steak knife, hands it to* WYNNE.

JACK  Best cutlery in the world.
WYNNE  My dad bought some of those knives offa QVC.

WYNNE *tries to hand the knife back.*

JACK  Oh, you can keep it. It's a sample.

WYNNE *drops the knife in his bag.*

*Stone Cold Dead Serious*                                                45

JACK *lights up, takes a hit from his joint, offers it to* WYNNE, *who declines.*

JACK  You sure you don't want a hit of this? It's Hawaiian.
WYNNE  I'm on a journey, dude. Tryin' to stay pure.
JACK  That's right, you're *journeying*.

JACK *takes another hit.*

JACK  So tell me about this journey.
WYNNE  You ever hear about Samurai warriors?
JACK  Weren't they those guys who would disembowel themselves?
WYNNE  It's called seppuku.
JACK  Seppuku, huh?
WYNNE  Yeah, man. It means to prove the purity of one's heart and soul. The truest Samurai is more afraid of shame than death. Seppuku is this totally noble act. It like protects your honor.
JACK  And how does that work exactly?
WYNNE  Let's say you ambushed my platoon and I was about to become your prisoner of war.
JACK  Okay.
WYNNE  Before you could get your shit-smeared paws on me I'd pull out my sword and perform seppuku.
JACK  I guess that would be honorable.
WYNNE  It would be the only option, man. Honor over everything else at all costs.
JACK  But what I always wondered was why do they have to slash away at their own stomachs with a sword? I mean, wouldn't it be easier to jump off a bridge or put a bullet in your head?

ADAM RAPP

WYNNE  The ancient Japanese believe that your soul exists in your abs.

JACK  Really?

WYNNE  Yeah, man. It's your spiritual center. So cutting your stomach like frees your soul.

JACK  But I can't imagine the suffering that would result from that. I mean, the blood and the gore. All your guts spilling into your lap.

WYNNE  You have to fight the fear, man.

JACK  And wouldn't it be hard?

WYNNE  Dude, it takes a huge will and the physical strength of an NFL lineman. But that's part of what makes it so honorable. The most popular way to do seppuku is called ZyumonziBara— crosscut style. According to my training master, this dude called a Kaisyakunin has to be present to cut off your head at the end of the ceremony.

JACK  What a job.

WYNNE  I know, right? And he better have a kick-ass sword or else things can get pretty gory.

JACK  So how does one actually *do* this seppuku thing?

WYNNE  You wanna know like step by step?

JACK  Just the general stuff.

WYNNE  Well, when you're all set up you sit erect with your legs folded under you on this mat thing called a tatami. In front of you is your wakizashi, which is a foot-and-a-half-long sword that makes your Cutco bullshit look small and sad. So when the moment of purity happens, you loosen your kimono and expose your abdomen—

JACK  My second wife had a kimono. She'd wear it around the house with nothing underneath. Go on.

WYNNE So when the moment of purity happens you expose your abdomen and seize your wakizashi and stab yourself at the lower left corner of your stomach and slowly cut across. Then you thrust all treacherous and vertical to the upper abs, and punctuate with a swift slice down toward your balls. As soon as this is done the Kaisyakunin dude chops your head off and your soul like totally leaps through your neck and gets to chill for the rest of time.

JACK Huh.

WYNNE Huh, what.

JACK I thought you said the Japs believe that your soul lives in your stomach.

WYNNE They *do*, dude. And it *does*. That's where you *free* it. It's *freed* there. But when it leaps out of you it goes through the gorge in your neck.

JACK Are you aware that your hair is blue?

WYNNE Um, yeah.

JACK How did that happen?

WYNNE I like dyed it. I'm actually gonna ask my girlfriend to shave my head tomorrow.

JACK Got a girly, huh?

WYNNE Yeah, dude.

JACK Is she this quote-unquote *friend* down in Crothersville?

WYNNE Um. Yes, actually. She is.

JACK What's her name?

WYNNE Sharice.

JACK Pretty name.

WYNNE I know, right?

JACK You like her a lot, huh?

WYNNE Yeah, man, she's my girlfriend. I love her.

JACK She good-lookin?

WYNNE  She's beautiful.

JACK  Nice figure?

WYNNE  Yeah. She's stacked, why?

JACK  Sharice, huh? I like that name a lot.

JACK *smokes, exhales.*

JACK  Can I ask you something, Danny?

WYNNE  What?

JACK  Does Sharice like to give you blow jobs?

WYNNE  *What?*

JACK  Blow jobs. Fellatio. You know what a blow job is, don't you?

WYNNE  Of course I do.

JACK  Huh.

WYNNE  What the fuck kinda question is that?

JACK  A pretty simple one, I'd say. *I* sure like em.

WYNNE  Are you like hinting at somethin, Jack?

JACK  I don't know, Danny, am I?

WYNNE  Dude, you're a total freak, aren't you?

JACK *slows down, pulls the car over.*

WYNNE  Why are you pullin the car over?

JACK  It's awfully wet out there.

*Only the sound of rain.*

WYNNE  Dude, I'll suck your dick for a hundred bucks, but I want the money up front and if you blow your load in my mouth I'll Cutco your fuckin balls off.

*Stone Cold Dead Serious*

JACK *pulls back onto the road. He reaches into his pocket and peels off a hundred-dollar bill, hands it to* WYNNE.

JACK  You ever done something like this before?

WYNNE  . . . Maybe.

JACK  I'm driving along and I see this kid and I says to myself I says now there's a young fella who's done something like this before.

WYNNE  So I'm sposed to do this while you're drivin eighty miles an hour?

JACK  I'll take her down to sixty-five. Just think of it as being part of the journey. And no teeth now or I'm taking fifty back.

JACK *undoes his pants and turns the radio back on: Herb Alpert & the Tijuana Brass this time.*

JACK  So . . . (*flipping tie over shoulder*) whenever you're ready.

WYNNE *stares down at his lap. Lights fade.*

## SCENE 3.

### THE LEDBETTERS.

CLIFF *is on the sofa watching QVC.*

LINDA ( *from off* ) Cliff, this saint stuff is just so interesting. Today Marna was telling the gals about St. Veronica. The story about this Veronica goes that when Christ was on his way to Golgotha he got tired and fell in the road and this woman—this Veronica gal—wiped his face with a towel. Apparently some sorta image of Jesus *remained* on the towel. Can you imagine that, Cliff? Gettin your towel back with a dang *face* on it? Now if that ain't miraculous I don't know what is.

I guess this Veronica became the patron saint of laundry workers and photographers. I swear to God, they got a patron saint for everything.

CLIFF *stands suddenly, teeters a bit, turns a full circle, as if he doesn't know where he is.*

LINDA ( *from off* ) I asked Marna if there's one for back pain. She was gonna look it up in her index thingy and tell me tomorrow.

CLIFF *takes his robe off, starts to fashion and hold the top part of it as if he is trying to hush a crying infant.*

LINDA (*from off*) She brought in a portrait of St. Dymphna, too. Oh, that Dymphna gal is so beautiful, Cliff. She looks just like Elizabeth Taylor in *National Velvet*. She's wearin this dress with puffy sleeves and she's holdin this pink rose. They put a glow around her head and everything.

CLIFF *lies down on the sofa, stomach first, and falls asleep, using his housecoat as a blanket.*

LINDA (*from off*) Marna didn't get into Dymphna's story cause she had to go pick up her daughter from choir practice, but she did say that this Dymphna gal is the patron saint of the insane and that you're sposed to pray to her if you think you or someone you love is goin crazy.

Dang, I wish I knew where that picture of St. Anthony of Padua was. I really wanted to show it to Marna. She don't believe me that he's holdin a sea bass.

SHAYLEE *appears at the head of the stairs. She is wearing a white nightgown. She is soaking wet and she has slit her wrists. There is also a gash in her leg and her dress is bloody. She is holding on to the paring knife. As she descends the stairs she starts to recite dinner grace.*

SHAYLEE In the name of the Father, the Son, and the Holy Spirit, Amen. Bless us O Lord for these Thy gifts which we are about to receive from Thy bounty through Christ our Lord, amen. Bless us O Lord for these Thy gifts which we are about to receive from Thy bounty through Christ our Lord, Amen . . .

SHAYLEE *crosses to the sofa, inserts the paring knife back into its slot in the block, and climbs on top of* CLIFF, *blanketing his sleeping body with hers.*

LINDA  Oh, there it is! How bout that! It musta fallen off the dang wall when we put the leaf back in the table—

LINDA *enters with the picture, sees* SHAYLEE *sprawled on top of* CLIFF, *blood seeping from her wounds, then drops the picture. Blackout.*

# ACT II

■　▦　■　▦

## SCENE 1.

### THE ST. MARK'S HOTEL.

*A hotel room in the East Village. A queen-sized bed. A TV. The walls are
filthy. A window overlooks a slightly seedy stretch of Third Avenue.*
SHARICE *is quietly seated on the bed. She is white, pretty. She wears
simple clothes and no makeup. She wears a small spiral notebook
around her neck. There is a pen attached by a string. There are two gym
bags in the corner.* WYNNE *paces by the window, staring out at the
street, coughing.* SHARICE *watches him.*

WYNNE Fuckin rain, huh? It's like it followed us here. How's
your neck?

*She rubs her neck, nods, smiles.*

WYNNE Yeah, sleepin on a bus ain't gonna do much for your
neck. Once when I was a kid I took Greyhound to Milwaukee
with my sister. There weren't any double seats open so I had to
sit next to this skinny black dude from New Orleans. He had this
huge fro and I accidentally fell asleep on his shoulder and when
we got to Milwaukee I woke up with a mouthful of jerry curl

juice. (*looks out the window, coughs*) I've never seen so many freaks. You heard what that chick in the hall said to me?

SHARICE *nods.*

WYNNE What a weirdo, right? . . . There's a guy out there pushing a duck around in a shopping cart. (*he coughs*)

SHARICE *takes out a cigarette, lights it.*

WYNNE You shouldn't smoke, Sharice. That shit'll kill you. My ma smoked for twenty years and her voice is fucked. This doctor did an X ray of her lungs and one of em was black. (*he coughs*) Like some bombed-out city in Europe.

*She smokes.*

WYNNE What time did that guy from *Tang Dynasty* say he was sposed to call?

SHARICE *opens her notebook, writes something, turns the page toward him. It reads:* SOON.

WYNNE Great. How soon is soon?

*He starts to pace, coughs.* SHARICE *turns the page, writes, taps on the pad to get his attention. He crosses to her, takes the pad.*

WYNNE (*reading from the pad*) Stop pacing. You're making me nervous . . . Sorry.

SNAKE LADY *enters from the bathroom. She is mid-forties, white. She wears a snakeskin vest and a fake boa constrictor around her neck. She wears red boots. She has a vast array of tattoos and chews a lot of gum.*

SNAKE LADY  Hey.

WYNNE  Hey.

SNAKE LADY  Who are yous two?

WYNNE  Um. Wynne and Sharice. Who are you?

SNAKE LADY  I'm Snake Lady. And this is Snake. Snake says hey.

WYNNE  Hey Snake.

SNAKE LADY  We share a bathroom.

WYNNE  We do?

SNAKE LADY  Yeah. I just thought I'd come through and welcome yas to the neighborhood.

WYNNE  Oh. Thanks.

SNAKE LADY  And Snake welcomes yas, too. First time in the Big Apple?

WYNNE  Um. Yeah.

SNAKE LADY  Yeah, you got that fresh look. New York's pretty weird, huh?

WYNNE  It's all right.

SNAKE LADY  Big buildings. Taxicabs. Psychopaths on every corner.

WYNNE *coughs convulsively.*

SNAKE LADY  That cough sounds serious.

WYNNE  It's just a cold.

SNAKE LADY  Raw garlic. I got a festoon of it in my room. You should come by. Eat a coupla cloves. Get a little freaky. You know what freaky is?

WYNNE  Um. Yeah.

SNAKE LADY  Yeah, I bet you do. You ever been freaked?

WYNNE  I've been freaked.

SNAKE LADY  What about your girlfriend, does she like to get freaked?

SHARICE *nods to* SNAKE LADY.

SNAKE LADY  If yous two wanna get freaky you've come to the right place. (*she starts dancing to some weird inner music*) A lot of very interesting vibrations are exploding offa Snake Lady's bod right now. Can you feel it, Glenn?

WYNNE  Wynne.

SNAKE LADY  (*still dancing*) Can you feel my vibes, Wynne?

WYNNE  Um, sure.

SNAKE LADY  Can I bum a cigarette, Eunice?

WYNNE  Sharice.

SNAKE LADY  Can I bum a cigarette, Sharice?

SHARICE *gives her a cigarette, lights her.*

SNAKE LADY  Thanks, love . . . You know we got the best bathroom on the floor?

WYNNE  Cool.

SNAKE LADY  But yous two got the Magnavox. Snake Lady's Trinitron jumps around so much it's like watching TV on a mechanical bull. I hope you appreciate the perks.

SNAKE LADY *crosses to the window, peers out.*

SNAKE LADY  I wish the freakin trailers would get here.

WYNNE  What trailers?

SNAKE LADY  The movie trailers. They're supposed to be settin em up on Cooper Square. Yous two got the classy view. The window in Snake Lady's room faces the courtyard. There's a pit bull chained to a tree. He's been eatin the tree for like three years.

WYNNE  Um, Mrs. Snake Chick or whatever your name is, I don't mean to be rude or anything, but what do you like, um, want?

SNAKE LADY  What do I want? I don't want nothin, Glenn.

WYNNE  Wynne.

SNAKE LADY  I don't want nothin, Wynne. Like I said, I just came through to welcome yas to the neighborhood. Snake Lady and Snake have lived in the St. Mark's Hotel for over twenty years. In room 4-G for gorgeous babe to be exact. A very important movie company is doing a documentary film about Snake Lady and Snake. They promised us a state-of-the-art honey wagon. (*she strokes* SNAKE *a bit*) Could I trouble you kids for some oil? Snake's gettin dry, Snake Lady needs to slick him down. Wesson oil. Coppertone. Crisco.

WYNNE  I'm sorry, but we don't got any oil, do we, Sharice?

SHARICE *shakes her head.*

SNAKE LADY  Why's she so quiet?

WYNNE  She only speaks when she feels like it.

SNAKE LADY  Why you so quiet, Sherry?

WYNNE  Sharice.

SNAKE LADY  Why you so quiet, Sharice, you afraida Snake?

WYNNE  Dude, I wouldn't fuck with her. She knows kung fu and she'll totally blaze a hole in your chest.

SNAKE LADY  Kung fu, huh?

SHARICE *nods.*

SNAKE LADY  Fancy, fancy. What part of the Midwest are yous two from, anyway? And don't tell Snake Lady you ain't from the Midwest cause you got that smell.

WYNNE  What smell?

SNAKE LADY  It's something between 7UP and caramel corn.

WYNNE *smells himself.*

SNAKE LADY  Smell it? 7UP and caramel corn. Farm boys and Catholic girls. Chevrolets in all the parking lots. Ain't you gonna ask me about my tattoos?

WYNNE  I wasn't like planning on it.

SNAKE LADY  What about you, Sherry?

WYNNE  Sharice.

SNAKE LADY  What about you, Sharice, you curious about Snake Lady's tats?

SHARICE *nods.*

SNAKE LADY  This one was done in '74 after Jack and the Silver Elephants played CBGB's. I got the spaceboy dragon twins at Tattoo and Cappuccino on St. Mark's between First and A. That was a very enlightening seven and a half hours. And Snake Lady just got her buns done on Tuesday but this gorgeous broad who stands before you ain't showin you her buns unless you got a king's ransom you're willin to part with.

WYNNE  What's that one?

SNAKE LADY  This one?

WYNNE  No, the one next to it. The one just above your bush.

SNAKE LADY  Oh, that's Saigo Takamori's sword. He was some Japanese hero.

WYNNE  Did you say Saigo Takamori?!

SNAKE LADY  Yeah, Saigo Takamori. You know who he is?

WYNNE  Dude, Saigo Takamori was the Last Samurai! He was like the greatest hero of modern Japan! He was a total badass!

SNAKE LADY  Good for him. Sounds like a interestin fella. If he ever comes to town I'd like to get together with him.

WYNNE  (*bemused*) It's a buke-zukuri koshirae. One of the finest weapons ever made. (*tracing the tattoo with his finger*) The hand manipulates the sword, the mind manipulates the hands. Cultivate the mind and do not be deceived by tricks, feints, and schemes. They are properties of the magician, not of the Samurai.

SNAKE LADY  Did Saigo Takamori say that?

WYNNE  No. Saito Yakuro said that. Saigo Takamori hardly ever spoke.

SNAKE LADY  Huh. All I know is it was the summer of '72 and Snake Lady was on this mescaline that was made in some basement on Great Jones Street and Snake Lady kept thinking she was a purple snow leopard who could speak Spanish— *Cuando estoy baracha mi español is mas major*—and she woke up two days later in a black van with Canadian plates just beyond the city limits of West St. Louis, Montana, and she had the tattoo.

*Stone Cold Dead Serious*

One of Snake Lady's old lovers who she refuses to go into detail about due to his untimely death running several hands of hashish out of the foothills of Little Honda, California, told her about Saigo Takamori and how it was his sword. This unnamed lover was a Zen Buddhist and he lived in a cherry-red '68 Vette with Florida plates.

WYNNE  Conquering evil, not the opponent, is the essence of swordsmanship. Yagyu Munenori.

SNAKE LADY *cocks her head oddly, listens for a moment.*

SNAKE LADY  Oh, no.
WYNNE  What.
SNAKE LADY  Snake just told Snake Lady that someone in this room's gonna die.
WYNNE  Really?
SNAKE LADY  Yes, I'd be careful if I was you. Snake rarely makes a mistake.

SHARICE *and* WYNNE *stare at each other.*

*The phone rings.*

SHARICE *and* WYNNE *stare at the phone.* SHARICE *nods at him to answer it, hands him the notebook and pen. He takes instructions down.*

WYNNE  *(into phone)* Hello? . . . *(he coughs)* Yeah, that's me . . . Uh-huh . . . Uh-huh . . . She's with me . . . He's not? . . . Oh. Why not? . . . Uh-huh . . . Uh-huh . . . Okay . . .

*While* WYNNE *takes his instructions down,* SNAKE LADY *crosses to* SHARICE, *stands over her.* SHARICE *reaches out and pets the snake.*

WYNNE (*to phone*) Hang on a second. (*to* SHARICE) They said the third finalist backed out and they wanna know if we're still gonna go through with it. It would be three against two . . . So you still wanna go through with it?

*She nods.*

WYNNE You sure?

*She crosses to* WYNNE, *kisses him on the mouth.*

WYNNE (*to the phone*) Yeah, we're still in . . . Okay. Later.

WYNNE *hangs up, coughs.*

SNAKE LADY You two involved in some kinda rumble?
WYNNE Yeah, you could say that.
SNAKE LADY Go for the knees. Snake Lady made it with a Abenacki Indian once. He said the weakest two spots on a man's body besides his balls are his knees. Kick em right in the kneecaps and take your bow. (*turning, looking out the window*) There they are. Finally. Snake Lady was startin to think this whole movie thing was a sham. Well, I'm gonna go check out my honey wagon. You get bored, Glenn, come knock on my door. It's the one with the big blue star on the front. Thanks for the cigarette, Sherry.

SNAKE LADY *exits. Silence.* WYNNE *coughs convulsively.*

WYNNE  So it's just gonna be me and you against three of those *Tang Dynasty* Broadswordsmen.

SHARICE *nods.*

WYNNE  The dude said we don't get our wakizashis till we show up. Some apartment on Tenth Street between First and A. Next to a Russian and Turkish bathhouse. (*he coughs*) This cold is fucking killing me, man. It's drainin all my mushin . . . Sharice, I'm scared for you, man.

*She pushes him.*

WYNNE  Sharice, on Sunday three *Tang Dynasty* Broadswordsmen are gonna try and kill us! I mean, I'm like scared for *myself*, and I'm a highly trained weapon of death. Are you sure you can handle this?

*With a quick burst,* SHARICE *effectively punches him in the stomach, taking him out. He lands on his back. She straddles him, on the floor.*

WYNNE  Okay, okay, okay.

SHARICE *thaws out of her strike pose, dips down, kisses him. She starts to hum.*

WYNNE  Dude, are you humming?

*She nods, hums.*

ADAM RAPP

WYNNE  You can hum?

*She nods, hums more.*

WYNNE  But you can't talk?

*She shakes her head, still humming.*

WYNNE  You didn't hum once on the bus.

*She finds her pad, writes.*

WYNNE  (*reading aloud from the pad*) I hum when I'm horny.

*He turns away, nervous.*

SHARICE *writes something on her pad.* WYNNE *reads it.*

WYNNE  Really?

*She nods.*

WYNNE  You really want me to do that?

*She nods.*

WYNNE  You ever like *done* that before?

*She shakes her head.*

WYNNE  Yeah, me neither.

*Stone Cold Dead Serious*

*She smiles.*

WYNNE  So we're like virgins.

*She nods.*

WYNNE  Wow. Samurai virgins.

*He laughs, coughs.* SHARICE *takes her shirt off.*

WYNNE  Whoa . . . You're like wearin a bra, man.

*They sit. They kiss, descend on the bed. Just as* WYNNE*'s back hits the mattress, he grabs the remote, turns on the TV to a rather involved porno.*

WYNNE  You ever watch this shit?

SHARICE *shakes her head. They move to the foot of the bed, watch for a moment.*

WYNNE  There's this one where this chick drives around in a Lamborghini and picks up hitchhikers and sucks their dicks for gas money. The weird thing is, you can't tell if she's suckin dick cause she likes it or if she really needs gas money. But on a symbolic level that's what sorta makes the movie work. Metaphors, you know? . . . I should prolly change this, huh?

SHARICE *nods.* WYNNE *changes the channel to QVC. The same two men from Act I scene 1 are narrating emphatic sales pitches about a Michael Jordan rookie card.*

WYNNE  My pop watches this shit. He's like totally addicted.
Sometimes he actually buys stuff. Once he bought a Christmas
tree. It was the middle of May. I came home from school and it
was set up in the living room. The fuckin thing was silver. My
ma was pissed for like six months.

He's all fucked up on pain pills, too. He's basically turnin
into the kinda person you can talk about when they're right
there in the room with you. About thirty percent actually
registers.

SHARICE *removes his shirt.*

WYNNE  I worry that you might think that I have a small dick or
somethin.

*She looks down his pants, gives him a thumbs-up, smiles.*

WYNNE  But do you think we like love each other, Sharice?

SHARICE *nods.*

WYNNE  Do you love me?

*She nods.*

WYNNE  Really?

*She nods, then gestures to him as if to say, "Do you love me?"*

WYNNE  Yeah, man, I love you. I love you so much, Sharice. I
couldn't stop thinkin about that the whole bus ride.

*Stone Cold Dead Serious*                                              67

*She kisses him passionately. They roll on the bed.* WYNNE *breaks from the kiss.*


WYNNE  But what happens if you start like bleeding? Maybe I should get some towels.


*She push-pulls him on top of her. They kiss more, roll again.* WYNNE *breaks away, crosses to the phone.*


WYNNE  (*while crossing*) I gotta call my ma.


WYNNE *grabs the phone, dials, waits.*


WYNNE  (*into phone*) Hey, Ma, it's me . . . Hey . . . Yeah, I made it (*he coughs*) . . . Yeah, I'm okay, it's just a cold . . . New York's a trip . . . How's Pop? . . . Uh-huh . . . Uh-huh . . . Just punch him in the balls, Ma, you were right, it totally works.
    Shaylee came home? . . . She what? . . . With Pop's Cutco? . . . Holy shit, is she okay? . . . Uh-huh . . . Uh-huh . . . Oh, shit . . .


*Wrapped in the sheet,* SHARICE *crosses to* WYNNE, *joins him on the floor next to the phone.*


WYNNE  (*into phone*) Don't cry, Ma . . . Ma, please stop cryin . . . Ma . . . Ma, listen to me. Tomorrow night is the *Tang Dynasty* Superchampionship and it's gonna be televised on Channel Thirty-seven. I want you and Pop to make sure and watch it, okay? . . . Nine o'clock . . . Promise me you'll watch it, Ma . . . You swear? . . . Okay, you two better watch it or I'll fuckin kill you. I'm puttin my ass on the line in a serious way here. And when I come home Pop can get that operation and I'll pay Shaylee's hospital bills and she can get clean and I'll start that computer business and we'll get central air and eat at the Sizzler every night, okay? . . . Okay, Ma? . . .

Are you gonna see Shaylee? . . . Well, if you see her, tell her she's so fuckin stupid but I love her . . . Okay, Ma . . . I gotta go, I love you, too.

*He hangs up, sits there a moment.*

WYNNE  Holy shit . . . My sister's in the hospital. She tried to kill herself.

She used to be a runner. She was like the best runner in Illinois. As a sophomore she won state in the mile and now she's a fuckin suicidal junkie prostitute. How the fuck does that even happen?

I mean, we used to do all this *stuff* together. When we were like kids. Once we made a snowman with tits and a Hercules boner and threw it off the roof. And another time we broke into our neighbor's house and pissed on their bed. For like no reason. We used to *do* stuff.

SHARICE *comforts him.*

WYNNE  Sharice, I want you to shave my head, okay?

*She nods.*

WYNNE  If I win I'm splittin the money with you.

*She gestures as if to say, "Me, too."*

*Stone Cold Dead Serious*                                                   69

WYNNE  But if I fuck up for some reason—like if I somehow lose my honor or I just plain suck—I want you to do somethin for me, okay?

*She nods.*

WYNNE  I want you to cut my head off before those *Tang Dynasty* fuckers can get to me. I'm gonna perform seppuku and I want you to be my Kaisyakunin.

*She nods.*

WYNNE  You promise?

*She nods, then gestures as if to say, "And you'll do the same for me?"*
WYNNE *nods, sits.*

WYNNE  Fuckin Shaylee . . .

SHARICE *lays next to him, covers them with the sheet. She comforts him.*

WYNNE  Hey, Sharice, can we like pretend we're Samurai warriors? Like I'm some young Samurai in trainin and you're Saigo Takamori and you're wearin this totally ancient-looking kimono with like dragons and tigers all over it?

*She nods, pushes him down on his back, starts to go down on him under the covers.*

WYNNE  And you're teachin me some totally unknowable shit about Zen. Like how when the cow drinks *wow* water it becomes

milk. And *wow* when *wow* a snake drinks *wow* water it *wow*
becomes poison *wow wow wow*—

*He looks under the covers.*

WYNNE  My boner's huge, man! I should like take a picture!

*She mounts him. They start to make love awkwardly, passionately.*
SHARICE *starts to hum as lights fade.*

# SCENE 2.

## MAPLE GROVE.

*A large white room with a thin, horizontal viewing window in the upstage wall.* SHAYLEE *lying asleep in a hospital bed. Her wrists are heavily bandaged and her arms are immobilized with straps. Her room is very clean and white.* CLIFF *is sitting in a chair under the TV, watching QVC with the sound turned down very low. He is wearing an old suit and his hair is combed severely. His hands are heavily bandaged. One of them may even be in a cast.* SHAYLEE *watches him for a long moment.*

SHAYLEE  Hey, Daddy.

*No response.*

SHAYLEE  I said hey.

*No response.*

SHAYLEE  Whatcha watchin?
CLIFF  They want five thou for a Michael Jordan rookie card. Who do they think we are, the German automotive industry?

ADAM RAPP

*He watches the TV.*

SHAYLEE  You can look at me, you know.

*No response.*

SHAYLEE  Hey, tough guy.

*No response.*

SHAYLEE  Too chicken to look, huh?
CLIFF  No.
SHAYLEE  Yeah.
CLIFF  No I ain't.
SHAYLEE  Yeah you are.
CLIFF  Nu-uh.
SHAYLEE  Yu-huh.
CLIFF  Screw you.
SHAYLEE  Screw you, fuckface. You won't even look at me.
You're a chicken.
CLIFF  I ain't no chicken!
SHAYLEE  Bawk-bawk.
CLIFF  I ain't no bawk-bawk!
SHAYLEE  Bawk-bawk, chickenshit.
CLIFF  You're the bawk-bawk!
SHAYLEE  You're the bawk-bawk!
CLIFF  I ain't afraida nothin! Except for water moccasins. Find
one in your canoe and you better know where you're sposed to
be.

*Only the TV.*

*Stone Cold Dead Serious*

SHAYLEE  I'm sorry, Daddy.

*No response.*

SHAYLEE  Did you hear me, Daddy? I said I was sorry.
CLIFF  I heardya.
SHAYLEE  Do you hate me?
CLIFF  No.
SHAYLEE  Yeah you do. You hate me.
CLIFF  No I don't either.
SHAYLEE  You won't look at me.
CLIFF  So?
SHAYLEE  Am I that ugly?
CLIFF  No.
SHAYLEE  Do I got snots in my nose or somethin?
CLIFF  No.
SHAYLEE  Crap in my teeth?
CLIFF  No.
SHAYLEE  Wanna fight?
CLIFF  No.
SHAYLEE  Cause I'll kick your ass, motherfucker.
CLIFF  Ha.
SHAYLEE  I'll kick you in the nuts and steal your lunch money.
CLIFF  Kick you in *your* nuts.

*Pause.*

SHAYLEE  What happened to your hands anyway?

*No response.*

SHAYLEE  Daddy, how'd you hurt your hands?

*He stares at his hands, turns to her.*

CLIFF  *(rising, crossing to upstage window)* Sometimes I wake up in the middle of the night and I don't know where I am. It's like I turn into . . . Like I'm . . .
SHAYLEE  Like you're what?
CLIFF  Like I'm nothin.
SHAYLEE  You're somethin, Daddy.
CLIFF  I'ma piece of meat.
SHAYLEE  No you ain't.
CLIFF  I'm meat that moves. I'm like ham.
SHAYLEE  You're Clifford Lemoyne Ledbetter of thirteen twenty-seven Rockland Drive. World-famous window glazier.

CLIFF *takes his pills out, considers them, puts them back in his pocket. He crosses back to his chair under the TV.*

SHAYLEE  Where's Ma?
CLIFF  She's down the hall.
SHAYLEE  What's she doin?
CLIFF  Talkin to the doctor.
SHAYLEE  Daddy, when I was asleep I had this dream.

*No response.*

SHAYLEE  You listenin, Cliff?

*He mutes the TV, turns to her.*

*Stone Cold Dead Serious*

CLIFF  I'm listenin.

SHAYLEE  I had this dream that I was little again. We were at the circus and my pants kept fallin down and I couldn't get em fixed right cause I had this big thinga cotton candy. And every time I'd go to eat it, it would turn into a bouquet of flowers.

When they brought the elephants out, my pants disappeared and I started eatin the flowers and it made you laugh.

CLIFF  You ate the flowers?

SHAYLEE  Yeah, and we weren't sad or nothin.

CLIFF  You ate em?

SHAYLEE  Yeah, I ate em.

CLIFF  Huh.

SHAYLEE  Did you hear me, Cliff? I said we weren't sad.

CLIFF  I heardya.

*Pause.*

SHAYLEE  Daddy, do you remember that time when me and Wynne made that snowman with the boobs and the Hercules boner and we threw it off the roof and you made us sit at the kitchen table for three hours cause you were so mad about us almost fallin off the roof?

CLIFF  Yeah.

SHAYLEE  And you sent me to my room until I apologized but I wouldn't apologize and later you came in to see if I was okay and I was hiding under my bed and cryin and I wouldn't come out until you sang that song about the three volcanoes. Do you remember that, Daddy?

CLIFF  Yeah.

SHAYLEE  I was just checkin.

CLIFF *watches QVC for a moment.*

SHAYLEE  Why you so dressed up, you goin to the prom or somethin?

CLIFF  Ha.

SHAYLEE  You're the Ha.

CLIFF  It's my old fishin suit. Used to wear to Lake Manteno. Manteno, Illinois. Catch more fish when you wear a suit. Bass mostly. Crazy about suits, them bass.

I took your mother fishin once. She wore her raincoat in the boat. I tried to get her to wear one of my JC Penny's Executive Man Ensembles with the matching power vest but she kept sayin she thought it made her look like Mayor Daley of Chicago, Illinois.

SHAYLEE  Did she?

CLIFF  Heck no. I thought she looked more like that guy who sells TVs at the Kmart. Dick Fryhoffen.

SHAYLEE  When I get outta here will you take me fishin? I'll wear one of your suits.

CLIFF  Bass fishin ain't like readin the phone book. It takes a steady hand.

SHAYLEE  What, you think I'm a idiot? I know I'm a worthless drug addict slut but I ain't no idiot.

LINDA *enters carrying flowers.* CLIFF *crosses back to the TV, sits.*
LINDA*'s hair is done and she is wearing a simple dress. There is a rosary wrapped around one of her hands. She sets the flowers down on the bedside stand, gently brushes* SHAYLEE*'s hair out of her eyes.*

LINDA  How you doin, baby girl?

SHAYLEE  Okay.

*Stone Cold Dead Serious*

LINDA  You was sleepin when we came in. Dr. Kennedy said you slept for fourteen hours yesterday. You feelin better?

SHAYLEE  A little. Why are you two so dressed up?

LINDA  Cause we went to church.

SHAYLEE  You guys went to church?

LINDA  We sure did, didn't we, Cliff? Our Lady of Good Councel in Aurora. Real nice people at that parish.

CLIFF  Priest looked like the Queen of Diamonds.

LINDA  Oh he did not either.

CLIFF  Did too. Harry the Queen of Diamonds. *Homo sapien* if I ever seen one.

LINDA  Father Harry ain't no homo, Cliff! He's a very nice man and he said some really important things about love and forgiveness and communication.

CLIFF  He kept singin the songs like he had to urinate. Kept makin this face. I thought he was gonna whip it out and piss right there on the antler.

LINDA  That's ridiculous, Cliff. And it ain't *antler* it's *altar.*

CLIFF  *Homo sapien* if I ever seen one.

LINDA  Shaylee, he told a parable about this little boy who kept cuttin down the olive trees and how after he got banished God appeared to him on a sacred rock and told him to repent and ask the people from his village for forgiveness and he did and then for the rest of his life he worked in the olive groves and pruned the trees and the olives flourished and he wound up helpin to make his village wealthy and they became famous for their olives.

CLIFF  Kid shoulda took the money and hightailed it to Mexico.

LINDA  Oh you!

CLIFF  Right down there at the Yucatán Peninsula. Fish tacos and square dancin all down the coast.

LINDA  I thought there was some real interestin messages in that story, Cliff. I thought his sermon was real thought-provokin.

CLIFF  Never did like olives, anyway. Things taste like cat food.

*Pause.*

SHAYLEE  Is that a rosary, Ma?

LINDA  It sure is.

SHAYLEE  Wow. Where'dja get it?

CLIFF  She bought it out of a gumball machine.

LINDA  Oh I did not either, Cliff. I got it from that Christian bookstore in Minooka.

CLIFF  She got it out of a gumball machine. Twenty-five cents. It was right there next to the SweeTarts and the jawbreakers. Kmart Blue Light Special.

LINDA  I got it last time we went down to visit you're Aunt Ricky, do-do brain. I'll show you a dang Blue Light Special.

CLIFF  Ha!

LINDA  You're the Ha! (*to* SHAYLEE) Don't your father look nice, Shaylee? When was the last time you seen him like this?

SHAYLEE  He looks like a porn star.

LINDA  No he don't either. I think he looks like Burt Lancaster.

CLIFF *suddenly stands, disoriented.*

LINDA  What wrong, Cliff? . . . You okay? . . . You need another diaper?

CLIFF *nods.* LINDA *reaches into her purse, hands him a diaper. He takes it, crosses to the bathroom as quickly as possible.*

*Stone Cold Dead Serious*                                                79

LINDA *mutes the TV, sets the remote on* CLIFF's *chair.*

LINDA  I ran into your track coach, Shaylee.

SHAYLEE  Who, Mr. Mecklo?

LINDA  He came into the restaurant with his family. He's got this little girl Winona. She's so cute. And his wife's real pretty. She's like showroom pretty. What a nice man, that Mr. Mecklo.

SHAYLEE  Yeah, real nice.

LINDA  What's wrong with him?

SHAYLEE  Well for one thing he fingerfucked Jane Baranowski behind the high-jumping mats.

LINDA  Oh he did not either.

SHAYLEE  He did so, Ma! He popped her cherry! He's disgusting! And he carries a picture of Muhammad Ali around in his pocket.

LINDA  Well I don't know nothin about that. All I know is he came into the restaurant the other day and he asked about you and he seemed real concerned.

CLIFF  (*from the bathroom*) Mahatma Gandhi was the greatest fighter that ever lived! Float like a bumblebee, sting like a sticka butter! Mahatma Gandhi!

LINDA  He said he thought he could help get you reinstated in school and maybe even back on the track team. I talked to Dr. Kennedy about it and he says that if you do all the group work and show a real interest in betterin your life and you keep recoverin that you might be ready to come home as early as the middle of September. And I talked to Principal Jeffcoat and she said she could work somethin out so that you could start doin schoolwork now so you wouldn't be too far behind when you went back. Not a bad deal, huh?

And you could make up more classes in the summer and maybe even graduate in August. Principal Jeffcoat said if things went well that you could prolly even walk across the stage with the rest of your class in June . . .

But you gotta *wanna* do this, Shaylee.

SHAYLEE  I do, Ma.

LINDA  I don't wanna lotta talk, now. You gotta start over for real this time. Get back on the good side of the track, you know? Dr. Kennedy said they got a new methadone program for kids and it's been real successful.

SHAYLEE  Methadone's for junkies, I ain't no junkie!

LINDA  Oh yeah, what are ya, a pharmacist?!

CLIFF  (*from the bathroom*) Come on, Lin, leave her alone. She said she was gonna put her shoulder in it.

LINDA  I know that's what she said, Cliff, but I just wanna reinforce the importance, you know? I mean, here she is, dehydrated, she lost all that blood, she's got goddang hepatitis!!!

SHAYLEE  Dr. Kennedy says it'll go away.

LINDA  Look how yellow you are! You're lucky you don't got AIDS, Shaylee! They tested you, you know!

SHAYLEE  I know.

LINDA  Usin needles! Screwin guys! You're really lucky!

SHAYLEE  I screwed a chick, too, Ma! This millionaire bitch from Barrington. Fucked her doggy style with a strap-on. It vibrated and it had veins!

LINDA  I don't wanna hear about that stuff right now—

SHAYLEE  And one night I smoked opium with this photographer I met down on Rush Street and we went into this van and I let him open me up with salad tongs. He took pictures of my cervix and sold em in Jewtown. And a lotta other really fucked-up shit happened, Ma! I lived in a laundry mat for a week!

LINDA  A laundry mat! Where the heck were you livin in a laundry mat?!

*Stone Cold Dead Serious*

SHAYLEE  In Gary.

LINDA  Oh for the love of . . .

CLIFF  (*after a pause, from the bathroom, singing*)
> *I've got three volcanoes*
> *Two are hot*
> *The other one is not*
> *But I keep my eye*
> *On that one as well*
> *Because with volcanoes*
> *You never can tell*

*Pause.*

LINDA  Are you're sure you even *wanna* come home, Shaylee?

SHAYLEE *nods.*

LINDA  And you'll go back to school and do your homework and help your father?

SHAYLEE *nods.*

LINDA  No more lyin, no more stealin?

SHAYLEE  No more lyin, no more stealin.

LINDA  You swear to God?

SHAYLEE  I don't believe in God.

LINDA  Why not?

SHAYLEE  Cause he's a dick. He's like the Easter Bunny and Santa Claus and Rumplestiltskin. The guy never shows up.

LINDA  Then give me your word.

SHAYLEE  I give you my word.

LINDA *sits in the chair opposite the TV, starts to cry.*

LINDA  You lived in a dang laundry mat?

SHAYLEE  It was only for a week. It was cool cause I knew how to steal candy outta the vending machine.

CLIFF *enters from the bathroom walking a little bowlegged.*

SHAYLEE  What happened to his hands?

LINDA  You want me to tell her, Cliff?

CLIFF  Wha?

LINDA  Shaylee wants to know what happened to your hands. You want me to tell her?

CLIFF  I don't care.

LINDA  He punched out all the windows.

SHAYLEE  When?

LINDA  The night you . . . After we came back from the hospital. He went from room to room and punched out the dang windows, the big gorilla.

CLIFF  You're the gorilla.

SHAYLEE  Daddy, why'd you do that?

CLIFF  I don't know. Felt like breakin stuff.

LINDA  Glass was every dang where. And now the house is all fulla mosquitoes.

CLIFF  I said I was gonna fix em.

LINDA  Yeah, you better.

*Pause.*

CLIFF  Shaylee had a dream about the circus. Cotton candy and the human cabbage ball. Confetti everywhere. Little kids runnin around. Everyone was happy, ain't it, Shaylee?

*Stone Cold Dead Serious*

SHAYLEE *nods.*

CLIFF  When my hands get better I'ma take Shaylee fishin.

LINDA  Well, that'll be interestin.

CLIFF  Takin her to Lake Manteno. Manteno, Illinois. We're gonna go bass fishin, ain't it, Shaylee? I'ma maker her wear her life saver, too.

LINDA  Life *preserver*, Cliff.

CLIFF  I'ma make her wear her life *preserver*, too. And if she takes it off I'ma make her put it back on.

LINDA  Well, whatever you do, don't let him make you wear one of those dang goofy suits.

CLIFF  Them suits ain't goofy.

LINDA  That's your best suit. The one you're wearin right now. Got it at TJ Maxx and it was a real good deal.

CLIFF *farts rather explosively.*

CLIFF  Goddamn leprechauns.

SHAYLEE *starts to laugh. Her laughter starts her coughing. She coughs convulsively for a moment.* LINDA *comforts her.* CLIFF *watches from the chair.*

LINDA  Shaylee, Marna gave me this beautiful picture of St. Barbara. She's sposed to be the patron saint of family tragedies. In the picture she's standin in front of a castle holdin this golden chalice. The story has it that her father got real angry after she converted to Christianity and he found her prayin in the forest and dragged her home by her hair and killed her. Well, God didn't like that none so he ordered her father to be struck by lightning.

The new cash register gal says Barbara's the patron saint of mine collapse, but Marna insists on family tragedy and she's the one with the index thingy. I hung it in your room, right over your trophy shelf.

*After a silence,* LINDA *checks her watch.*

LINDA  Oh crymie, Cliff! Change the channel! Wynne's gonna be on TV. Channel Thirty-seven! It prolly already started. Quick, Cliff!

CLIFF *switches the channel to Thirty-seven. An announcer with a boisterous Australian accent is speaking.*

ANNOUNCER  (*voice-over*) Mr. Ledbetter, you're from Chicago, Illinois, is that right?
LINDA  Turn it up, Cliff!

CLIFF *adjusts the volume.*

WYNNE  (*voice-over*) Yeah. Well, actually Norridge, which is just north of the city.
ANNOUNCER  (*voice-over*) And in September you'll be entering you junior year in high school, is this correct?
WYNNE  (*voice-over*) Yeah. Norridge High School. Go Rams.
ANNOUNCER  (*voice-over*) And do you have family back in Norridge?
WYNNE  (*voice-over*) Yeah. There's my ma, Linda, my pop, Cliff,

and my sister, Shaylee. They're prolly watching right now. Hey, Ma. Hey, Pop. Hey, Shaylee. Shaylee, you're stupid as fuck for what you did but I love you anyway.

ANNOUNCER  (*voice-over*) And Wynnewood Jericho Ledbetter, do you feel you're ready for tonight's Superchampionship?

WYNNE  (*voice-over*) As ready as I'll ever be. When a cow drinks water he becomes milk. When a snake drinks water he becomes poison.

ANNOUNCER  (*voice-over*) And what would you do with one million dollars?

WYNNE  (*voice-over*) I'm gonna pay off the mortgage on our house back in Chi, take care of this operation my pop needs for his back, and give a chunk to my sister Shaylee so she can get her life back together.

ANNOUNCER  (*voice-over*) And what exactly is wrong with your sister?

WYNNE  (*voice-over*) She's just a little screwed up right now.

ANNOUNCER  (*voice-over*) Fair enough, Mr. Ledbetter. And how have you been preparing for today's event?

WYNNE  (*voice-over*) Well, for the past six months I've been training with Slice, my kendo master. What's up, Slice?

ANNOUNCER  (*voice-over*) And you feel you're comfortable with the wakizashi?

WYNNE  (*voice-over*) Dude, I'm more than comfortable with it. I *am* it. As it is me.

ANNOUNCER  (*voice-over*) Excellent answer! And one last question, Wynnewood Jericho Ledbetter of North Chicago, Illinois: Rumor has it that you and your fellow finalist, one Miss Sharice Williford of Crothersville, Indiana, are romantically involved. Is this indeed true?

WYNNE  (*voice-over, coughing*) Yeah, man. Sharice is my girl. I love her. She's a badass kung fu master and those *Tang Dynasty* dudes better watch out. If one of us wins, we're splitting the money.

ANNOUNCER (*voice-over*) And here she is now. Miss Sharice Williford of Crothersville, Indiana. Is this true, Miss Williford? Do you intend on splitting your prize money with Mr. Wynnewood Jericho Ledbetter of North Chicago, Illinois?

WYNNE (*voice-over*) Um, she's not much of a talker.

ANNOUNCER (*voice-over*) No, I guess she's not. But we did get a nod, ladies and gents!

So there you have it: a young bloke from the North Side of Chicago, Illinois, and his Indiana girlfriend, a kung fu master with a lot of intensity but not a lot to say! This is a challenge to the death, ladies and gents! Both finalists have loads to lose but even more to gain! When we come back we'll get right down to it: The *Tang Dynasty* Superchampionship! A winning purse worth *one million dollars!*

*A cottage cheese commercial.* LINDA *crosses to* CLIFF, *takes the remote, mutes the TV.*

CLIFF Wha?

LINDA Neat huh? Wynne looks good with his head shaved, ain't it?

CLIFF He looks like that guy in the toilet.

LINDA What guy in the toilet?

CLIFF The Tidy Bowl Man.

LINDA No he don't either, Cliff. The Tidy Bowl Man wears a dang sailor's cap. You're thinkin of Mr. Clean. What do you think, Shaylee?

SHAYLEE I think somethin bad's gonna happen.

LINDA *unmutes the TV. Back to the show.* CLIFF *moves his chair to the other side of* SHAYLEE's *bed, sits.*

ANNOUNCER (*voice-over*) And we're back, ladies and gents! Live, from an undisclosed location in New York City's East Village, it's the *Tang Dynasty* Superchampionship, where two young lovers will take on three professional mercenary Broadswordsmen! Wynnewood Jericho Ledbetter and Sharice Williford have been given their wakizashis and are poised, back to back, awaiting the onslaught of the three kendo masters, who will appear one at a time! Will they come through the window? Or from down that hallway? Will they come out of the bloody bathroom? Nobody knows! It's just like the video game, only now it's real live life and death!

And here comes the first one—Zhang Yun Chen! He simply walked into the room, can you believe that?! Very unlike the video game! Look at those legs! Those arms! What power! What unbelievable confidence! And there they go! Zhang attacks Sharice high, low, high, low! He's got Sharice off her mark. She's losing her foothold! But here comes Wynnewood Jericho Ledbetter from North Chicago, Illinois, who counters with his wakizashi! High, low, high, low! You can see the sparks flying off their swords! And Sharice Williford is back on her feet and they have Zhang Yun Chen cornered! And there's a clean blow to the midsection! Zhang Yun Chen is down! Look at all that blood! If that's not a fatal blow I don't know what is!

And what's this, ladies and gents!? Jack Li Foi, also known to kung fu aficionados as The Future, has just crashed through the street-facing window and he is wielding his infamous Three Powers Sword! He goes right for Wynnewood Jericho Ledbetter

ADAM RAPP

of North Chicago, Illinois! The flash of the Three Powers is blinding, ladies and gents! Our camera crew is in awe! Cameras up, boys! Back into the fray! Jack Li Foi hurls his Three Powers at Mr. Ledbetter! Ledbetter counters with his wakizashi once, twice, thrice! Jack Li Foi comes at him again, this time attacking the lower torso, but Ledbetter counters! Can you hear that clanging! It's unbelievable! And now Sharice Williford has thrown herself into the mix! And what's this! Pepper spray! Good old-fashioned pepper spray! A quick spritz to the eyes and Foi is down! He's begging for mercy, ladies and gents, down on his hands and knees, pleading with Sharice Williford of Crothersville, Indiana, like a bloody baby! And it appears that Miss Williford is actually going to *spare* the bloke!

LINDA AND SHAYLEE NO!

ANNOUNCER (*voice-over*) There's no room for mercy when one million dollars is on the line. Take him out, Sharice! Drive your sword into his jugular!

LINDA AND SHAYLEE DO IT!

ANNOUNCER (*voice-over*) But wait! At long last! Lo and behold! Straight off the fire escape! The moment we've been waiting for, ladies and gents! The man with the golden sun on his chest! It's Gao Mein Jian and he's wielding twin Wushu nine-ring broadswords! There are two swords flying from one bloke, ladies and gents! And before you can say who-what-when he's on top of Sharice Williford of Crothersville, Indiana, and she's fallen on top of the blubbering Jack Li Foi! And look at Foi! A moment ago he was begging for his life and now he's collaborating with Gao Mein Jian! How quickly things turn! And Jian strikes! Once! Twice! Thrice! And there goes her head! Ladies and gents, Gao Mein Jian has *beheaded* Miss Sharice Williford of Crothersville,

Indiana, with the blazing fury of double Wushu nine-ring broadswords! And what's this?! Gao Mein Jian is down as well! Gao is down! He's down, ladies and gents! And Ledbetter is clutching his Taser gun! It appears that he has actually Tasered Gao Mein Jian! It doesn't get any better than this!

Wynnewood Jericho Ledbetter, the young giant slayer from North Chicago, Illinois, has felled perhaps one of the greatest living kung fu masters! And now Ledbetter is measuring off his final fatal blow! Ladies and gents if you're faint of stomach I'd advise getting to your nearest W.C.! The five-time kung fu champ is dead and the golden sun on his chest is awash in crimson! And now Ledbetter is measuring off on Jack Li Foi! I highly doubt that there will be mercy involved in what you are about to see, ladies and gents! And—*oooof*—there it is! Inevitability! Destiny! A head for a head, as it were!

Wynnewood Jericho Ledbetter of North Chicago, Illinois, is indeed our true, real-life *Tang Dynasty* Superchampion! And here he is now, kneeling before his dead beloved! Oh the bloody cruelty of the world! The fight marshals have confiscated his wakizashi!

Ladies and gents, Sharice Williford's head has literally rolled out of the frame and Wynnewood Jericho Ledbetter of North Chicago, Illinois, is on his knees, seemingly praying to her nogginless corpse!

And what is this?! From some unknown fold of his kimono Mr. Ledbetter has produced what appears to be a small knife and he's attempting to disembowel himself! Could he be performing the legendary Samurai warrior's seppuku, more commonly known in layperson's terms as hari-kari?!

The fight marshals are all over him! And they've located the knife! His stomach is bleeding! Somebody call an ambulance! Somebody call an ambulance! For the love of God, will somebody please—

*A long beep.* LINDA *grabs her purse, sprints out of the room.* CLIFF *goes after* LINDA, *moving as fast as he can.*

*Lights fade as* SHAYLEE *lays back in the bed, staring straight ahead.*

## SCENE 3.

### MAPLE GROVE.

*The same room, one week later.* WYNNE *is lying in bed, watching QVC with the sound turned down very low. His head is shaved and there is a large blue star tattooed to the top of his skull. His stomach is heavily bandaged. He is in extreme pain, can only communicate by writing with a marker on a spiral notebook, which rests on the bedside stand. It's the same notebook that* SHARICE *was using in Act II, scene 1.* WYNNE's *arms are strapped down. There is an IV connected to one arm and a tube in his mouth. There is a pitcher of water, a cup, and a large flexible straw placed next to his bed.* SHAYLEE *eases into the room. She's wearing a white hospital gown and holding a small paperback book. She is nervous, a bit tentative, somehow eager.*

SHAYLEE  Hey.

WYNNE *looks over.*

SHAYLEE  How's it goin?

*He gestures vaguely.*

ADAM RAPP

SHAYLEE  Cool haircut.

*No response.*

SHAYLEE  Is the tattoo real?

*He nods.*

SHAYLEE  Did it hurt?

*He nods.*

SHAYLEE  Your skull is weird. It makes you look like you got a
huge brain. Freaky genius boy . . .
 This was my room, you know? . . . You better treat it good.
No pissin the bed . . .
 So there's like a zillion reporters downstairs. You're all
famous and shit. They're callin you nicknames. Wynne the
Winner. The Samurai Wonderboy. The Kendo Kid . . .
 So this place is pretty wack, ain't it? Prolly never thought
you'd wind up in a fuckin loony bin? Ugly doctors and fat nurses.
You should see the sixth floor. It's just the opposite. Food sucks,
too. You try the chipped beef yet?

WYNNE *shakes his head.*

SHAYLEE  Tastes like dogshit. Chipped beef on Tuesday, hoagies
on Wednesday. Pot pies every Thursday.

*Awkward silence.* SHAYLEE *looks around, unsure of herself.*

SHAYLEE  I'll bet you beat your meat to all the nurses.

SHAYLEE *mimes* WYNNE *beating his meat for a moment, tries to make him laugh.*

SHAYLEE  Check it out.

*She shows him the book:* Franny and Zooey.

SHAYLEE  It's the only book I've ever finished. It's about this fucked-up family from New York. This guy from group gave it to me. We made out in the commons room after this crack addict chick played the guitar. His name is Blacky. Cool name, huh? His real name's Marcus. He's from Harwood Heights. He's court-appointed. He accidentally killed his little brother in a drunk-drivin accident. He's got crooked teeth and he sort of smells but he's cute as shit . . .
    Maybe you could read the book?

*She places the book on his chest.*

SHAYLEE  Your girlfriend was so pretty. She was like showroom pretty.

WYNNE *starts to cry, tries to bust out of the straps, nearly lifting out of the bed, collapses.* SHAYLEE *calms him.*

SHAYLEE  (*singing*)
    *I've got three volcanoes*
    *Two are hot*

*The other one is not*
*But I keep my eye*
*On that one as well*
*Because with volcanoes*
*You never can tell*

SHAYLEE *remains standing, tries not to fidget.*

SHAYLEE Wynne, you know about six months ago I had a baby? It came out dead. It was about the size of a tomato. I put it in a McDonald's bag and threw it in the garbage. I talked about it in group today. How I keep dreamin about it. How sometimes it's huge and it's eatin hamburgers at that Wendy's Oasis on 294. How I always wake up all fucked up and cryin.

This nun told me that God's tryin to talk to me and that I should use the opportunity to ask Him for forgiveness. Like I should start prayin and shit.

In group we had to go around a circle and describe our own personal picture of God. The crack addict chick said God was Smokey the Bear. I said he's like this old freak wrapped in a shower curtain and he's got this big holy boner. And he's eatin one of those side salads from Kentucky Fried Chicken.

Blacky was all, "Naw, man, God's a meat eater." His personal picture of God is this old buff ancient-lookin fucker in a toga. And he's got a perm and he's at the Sizzler eatin a steak. Pretty funny, ain't it? . . .

Group's pretty cool. You get to talk about yourself, you know? Listen to all these fucked-up stories. Some people just sit there. You don't even gotta say nothin if you don't wanna . . .

In the book there's this whole thing about God, but it ain't all phony. The brother calls him the Fat Lady. It's actually pretty cool, Wynne. They learn about stuff, you know? Like how to get through the shitty times . . .

Ma's talkin about you like you're her hero. She paid off the house yesterday. And Pop's seein this back specialist in Mount Prospect. And I guess Marna's husband's gonna come over and look at the house to see about central air.

Pop's callin you the Champ. They're on their way right now . . .

Dr. Kennedy said I can go home next month. I might do this halfway house thing first, but I'd get to crash at home on the weekends. Urine samples every three days. Try your luck, piss in a cup.

Ma says I've been approved to re-enroll at Norridge, too. If I catch up in school they're gonna let me back on the track team. Mr. Mecklo asked me to run the mile again but I was like, fuck that, I wanna pole-vault. Fly over some shit, you know? . . .

I'm gonna stay clean this time, Wynne, I really am . . .

So what about you? What are you gonna do when you get outta here? Any big plans? Ma says you're gonna start some computer company.

WYNNE *gestures toward the notebook and marker.* SHAYLEE *hands it to him, undoes his straps so he can write.* WYNNE *writes* **MY PILLOW.** SHAYLEE *reads.*

SHAYLEE  Your pillow? . . . You need me to adjust it?

WYNNE *writes.* SHAYLEE *looks.*

SHAYLEE  (*reading from pad*) Smother me.

SHAYLEE *watches him for a moment, confused, her hands trembling. She takes the pillow from under his head, stares at it for a moment, crosses to the other side of the bed, stays there for a moment, raises the pillow, can't do it, lowers the pillow.*

SHAYLEE Hey Wynne, you know that tree we used to drive by when we'd go down to Kankakee? That willow tree where they sell the pumpkins during Halloween? Pop would always stop the car and make us get out and race around it? I wanna go there and just like sit under it for a while. Listen to the cars go by. Fall asleep, you know? . . .

After we get outta here I'm takin you there, okay? Grass, and shit like that . . .

Cause I just want us to be happy again. And not just not-sad. Happy.

*She gets in the bed with him, then takes his hand as if to keep herself from shaking. They stare at each other for a long time. Grandaddy's "Underneath the Weeping Willow" plays as lights slowly fade.*

# FASTER

■  ▦  ■  ▦

*Faster* was originally produced in New York City by the Rattlestick Theater Company (David Van Asselt, Artistic Director) at the Rattlestick Theater on September 9, 2002. It was directed by Darrell Larson; sets were designed by David Korins; costumes by Kaye Voyce; lights by Jeff Croiter; and sound by Eric Shim. The production stage manager was Lori Ann Zepp. The cast was as follows:

| | |
|---|---|
| STARGYL | *Robert Beitzel* |
| KITCHIN | *Mtume Gant* |
| SKRAM | *Chris Messina* |
| MAN | *Roy Thinnes* |
| GIRL | *Fallone McDevitt Brooking* |

# CHARACTERS

STARGYL     *white, seventeen, starving, a mute*

KITCHIN     *black, barely twenty, starving, a dreamer*

SKRAM     *white, barely twenty, starving, a glue huffer, Stargyl's*
           *older brother*

MAN     *white, fiftyish, playful, terrifying*

GIRL     *a child from the river*

# SETTING

The basement room of a condemned apartment house. Summer.

# ACT I

■　▦　■　▦

*Twilight.*

*The basement room of a condemned apartment house. A forgotten room.*
*Malarial, spoiled walls. A crooked, half-collapsed staircase. A small,*
*ceiling-level, foot-high drain window facing the street. A half-carpeted*
*cement floor. Dirt. A door leading to a boiler room. A padlock securing*
*the door.*

*Two thick heavy bag chains dangling from the ceiling, a large hook at*
*the end of each chain. An ancient boxer's heavy bag leaning in one*
*corner. Two makeshift sleeping nests against opposite walls. A metal*
*sink. A broken section of mirror above the sink. A small jar of hair*
*pomade next to the spout. A flashlight under the sink. An old radio*
*whose reception phases in and out. A few wooden crates turned upside*
*down as makeshift furniture. Several voided tubes of airplane glue*
*scattered about the room. Random empty milk cartons and Count*
*Chocula cereal boxes litter the floor. Strange squares torn in the milk*
*cartons. A large plastic pink beach pail. A stack of newspapers neatly*
*piled in one corner. The room is lit by a single filthy, naked bulb hanging*
*from the center of the ceiling. A cheap transistor radio spits static and*
*occasional decipherable bits.*

RADIO   *Florida orange juice on ice*
        *Sounds so nice*
        *In the morning*

*Florida orange juice on ice*
*Tastes so fresh*
*The day is dawning*

*Florida orange juice*
*Healthy start*
*To a brand new day*

*Florida orange juice*
*Vitamin C*
*It's the sunshine way*

STARGYL *is standing in the corner opposite the door to the boiler room.*
*He is tall and thin, boyish. He is surrounded by a small shrine of green*
*plastic toy soldiers. He is arranging them on the floor in various warfare*
*poses, carefully removing them from a shoebox. He is dressed in a tattered*
*seersucker suit, a white T-shirt underneath the jacket. He wears old high-*
*top sneakers, electric tape wrapped around the soles. On one hand he*
*wears three plastic toy rings; cereal box prizes. Set neatly at his feet is a*
*pair of enormous fire-engine-red pumps. He is sweating profusely. He*
*occasionally barks at the flickering light. It is muffled but definitely a*
*bark, more human than dog-like. The light continues to flicker. He covers*
*his face with both hands as if trapped in a terrible storm. Outside, a*
*broadcast public service announcement from a "Heat Relief" van.*

BROADCAST  ATTENTION, ATTENTION. THIS IS THE
AGENCY FOR HEAT RELIEF. IN LIGHT OF THE PRESENT
CONDITIONS, DO NOT—I REPEAT—DO *NOT* PHYSICALLY
EXERT YOURSELF. HEAT STROKE AND GENERAL
EXHAUSTION ARE SERIOUS THREATS TO YOUR HEALTH.

ADAM RAPP

*The sound of descending footfalls.*

KITCHIN *enters from the staircase. He is black, barely twenty, thin. He wears a Chicago Bears football jersey and absurdly long basketball shorts. He has crude tattoos about his arms. On his feet he wears Nike basketball shoes. On his head, a do rag. He carries a load of newspapers, a shoeshine box on top of the papers. He dumps his load, taps the light. It stops flickering.*

KITCHIN  Yo, Stargyl, it's like a furnace out there. Sidewalk crackin. Street breathin up your legs. Can't even get no breeze from them big church fans at St. Jack's. Feels like a *dog's* lickin you. Niggas sittin in the pews lookin like they meltin and shit. Women in they bras. Men naked from the waist up. Everyone starin at Jesus like he gonna do somethin about it. You know someone spray-painted that nigga blue? A blue motherfuckin Jesus. Like he a Smurf or some shit. That ain't right, Stargyl. This heat brings out the craziest shit in people. Liable to make a brother jump right in the river.

*The light flickers again.* STARGYL *whimpers.*

KITCHIN  Bellerin like a dog. It ain't nothin but a little light flickerin. You act like it's aliens or some shit.

STARGYL *tries to force his hand in his mouth.*

KITCHIN  Get your hand out your mouth.

STARGYL *takes his hand out of his mouth.*

KITCHIN  All you gotta do is tap that joint.

KITCHIN *picks up one of the milk cartons, tears the lost child's photograph off the back panel, stares at it, takes a rubber-band-bound bunch of other milk carton photographs out of his pants, joins the new one with the others, stuffs the bunch down his pants.*

KITCHIN  Pay phone ring?

STARGYL *shakes his head.*

KITCHIN  Yeah, that joint don't never ring. Skram said that nigga from Oswego's sposed to call.

KITCHIN *picks up an empty tube of airplane glue, throws it against the wall.* STARGYL *starts to arrange his green plastic soldiers.*

KITCHIN  Yeah, play with your army, Stargyl. Be all you can be and shit.

STARGYL *plays. Static from the radio.*

KITCHIN  Yo, you been keepin lookout?

STARGYL *nods.*

KITCHIN  Defendin and watchdoggin? Woof-woofin like a good hound?

STARGYL *nods, barks a few times.*

KITCHIN  You didn't see no five-oh, did you? No pigs and chickens?

STARGYL *shakes his head.*

KITCHIN  None of them department of everlastin assbustin motherfuckas?

*A knocking from behind the boiler room door.*

KITCHIN  It was Skram's turn to feed her. Punk-ass nigga never even came home last night. Knucklehead prolly got caught chasin paste. We was sposed to meet up at the train station. Trick a load of *Tribunes*. Talkin bout meet me at seven-thirty. Don't be late. Don't be a sucka. Motherfucka talkin about time in the a.m. and don't even got no watch!

Skram poppin off about gettin fifty heads from the janitor at the newspaper and shit. Sell em over at the train station to them rich white niggas on they way to Chi. I'm standin next to the switch house holdin a armful of yesterday's *Trib* lookin like I'm homeless and shit!

And you can't trick them white niggas twice cuz once they get to New Lennox they'll see it's yesterday's paper. Train hits Blue Island and they already callin the po-lice on they space phones.

Headlines is like the same every day, anyways. The heatwave this. The reservoir that. Old folks dyin in fronta they fans. Skeighty-eighth day of no rain. Shit is gettin mad boring, yo. Motherfuckas get tired of readin bout the same old news. Lucky if we was to sell *half* them joints . . .

Skram's frantic ass! Janitor at the newspaper prolly busted him in the head with a pushbroom.

Got my fitty from Big Cheese at the Copley printin press. Shine up his shoes and he always comes through for a brother. Got my fitty!

KITCHIN *picks up a few empty boxes of Count Chocula, pours the dregs into the beach pail, stares at the small accumulation.*

KITCHIN Skram's fiendin-ass ate all the cereal again.

*Another knock.*

KITCHIN *picks up another tube of glue, throws the tube against the wall, more agitated. The light flickers again.*

KITCHIN You want the water?

KITCHIN *grabs the plastic beach pail off the floor, crosses to the sink, dumps the cereal dregs, fills the pail with water. He crosses to* STARGYL, *holds the pail at his side.* STARGYL *reaches toward the pail with his ringed hand.*

KITCHIN Other hand, Stargyl. You wanna mess up your spook rings? Them joints won't glow right you get em wet.

STARGYL *hesitates.*

KITCHIN Go head on and float your hand.

STARGYL *places his other hand in the pail.* KITCHIN *swirls the water.*

KITCHIN  That feel good?

STARGYL *nods.*

KITCHIN  I know it do. Like you in the pool over at Inwood.
Jumpin off the divin board. Sinkin down like you floatin through
space. Touchin the bottom. All them locker keys caught in the
drain. Maybe you see a quarter. You feelin it, right?

STARGYL *nods.*

KITCHIN  Yeah, B. (*swirling the water*) Star-gyl. Stargyl Super*star*!

KITCHIN *stops swirling the water.*

KITCHIN  You straight?

STARGYL *nods.*

KITCHIN  You frontin?

STARGYL *shakes his head emphatically.*

KITCHIN  No more actin like a little bitch, now. You start up
again and I'll make you sit in the punk crate. Make you sit in that
joint till Skram gets back, you hear?

STARGYL *nods.* KITCHIN *crosses to the sink with the pail, dumps the*
*water.* STARGYL *continues arranging his soldiers.* KITCHIN *crosses to*
*a gym bag, gathers the small parts of his life, begins packing.* STARGYL
*walks over, tries to stop him.*

KITCHIN  What?

STARGYL *points to his bag.*

KITCHIN  Ain't nobody gonna leave you behind—you
straight . . . (*packing*) You packed up and ready to roll?

STARGYL *nods.*

KITCHIN  Got your comb?

STARGYL *reaches into his pocket, removes a comb.*

KITCHIN  Your lighter?

STARGYL *reaches into his other pocket, removes a Zippo lighter.*

KITCHIN  Star-*gyl*! Look at you! Tonight's the night, B. All
this shit'll be settled. Finally pay off that Buick Electra two-
twenty-five over on Gompers. Buck and a half and it's
ours. Two bills and Fat Rick throws in a extra set of
Michelins.
       Money let me push that joint today. Shit was mad lovely, yo!
Pleather interior. Electric seats. Power windows. Four-forty
engine. Horse power buzzin all through my ribcage. Niggas was
like, *Whaddup, Kitchin? Where you get the ride, yo? Lemme sit
shotgun,* and whatnot. Joint felted like I was ridin in some mad
*waterbed* type shit.
       Finally get the fuck off the East Side. Word is bond,
Stargyl. So long as that nigga from Oswego come
through.

STARGYL *starts to comb his hair.*

KITCHIN  Yeah, go head and do your hair. You do it good enough I'll give you some relaxer, bet?

STARGYL *combs with concentration.*

KITCHIN  Star-*gyl*! Stargyl Super*star*! Comb that shit, dog! Bust them naps!

KITCHIN *crosses to the sink, grabs a small jar of pomade, applies it to* STARGYL*'s hair.*

KITCHIN  Skram says New York City but I say we lay it down in Florida.
     You ever seen Florida on the map, Stargyl? It look like a dick, B. Like big black donkey dick. Only they always make that joint yellow cuz of all the oranges and shit. They got mad vitamin C down there . . .

KITCHIN *finishes with* STARGYL*'s hair, picks up another box of cereal, peers inside.*

KITCHIN  I'm starvin like marvin. Feels like motherfuckin cats is cryin in my stomach.
     When I was at St. Jack's Father Freeman told this Bible story about how Jesus made a school of fish appear in this dead river so all these homeless bummy-type niggas could eat. That sounds pretty dope, don't it, Stargyl?

STARGYL *nods, still combing his hair.*

*Faster*

KITCHIN  He said you can say this prayer. Somethin, somethin, I shall not want. The Lord is my Suburban or my Chevrolet or some shit. He said if you say it over and over it'll take that hunger away.

KITCHIN *crosses to the boiler room door, presses his ear to it, then pushes away and starts walking frenetically around, like a caged animal, saying, "The Lord is my somethin but I shall not want. The Lord is my somethin but I shall not want," under his breath, clutching his sides.* STARGYL *combs his hair faster and faster, trying to keep pace with* KITCHIN.

*Again, outside a broadcast public service announcement from the "Heat Relief" van.*

BROADCAST  ATTENTION, ATTENTION. THIS IS THE AGENCY FOR HEAT RELIEF. DUE TO THE CURRENT DRAUGHT, WATER LEVELS THROUGHOUT THE CITY ARE AT AN ALARMINGLY LOW LEVEL. PLEASE DO NOT— I REPEAT—*DO NOT* FLUSH YOUR TOILET UNTIL FURTHER NOTICE.

KITCHIN *crosses to the sink, lowers his head over the faucet, lifts his do-rag, runs cold water over the back of his neck, stops the faucet, then crosses to the window, jumps up, grabs the ledge, pulls himself up, peers out.*

KITCHIN  Come on, Skram! . . . Where is that nigga?! Fiendin-ass pastehead.

KITCHIN *lets himself down, picks up a box of Count Chocula, shakes it, drops the box, picks up another, shakes it, throws it to the floor.*

KITCHIN I don't know about that nigga, sometimes, Stargyl. Got all these ideas, but don't none of them ever work out. Snatchin headlines. Jukin quarters from pay phones. Scrappin carparts over on Plainfield Road.

Don't none of it ever pay. And if it do it ain't shit but enough for a train ticket to Chi. We get there we can't do nothin cuz we broke. Wind up ridin the El all night. Memorizin all the stops on the Red Line. Knowin them joints backwards and shit. Thinkin about gettin a drink. Gettin some ass. Nothin but them South Side hos on the train stankin up the seats with they rotten pussies.

Shoulda spent the summer in Rock Island with my cousin Two Tone. Sells T-shirts out the back of his Nova. Mickey Mouse and shit. I'm with stupid and whatnot. At least people buy them joints. Two Tone's got a tough little crib, too. Color TV. Microwave. Nice hot shower.

Rock Island woulda been better than this shit. Always waitin around for nothin. Growin old like them lopsided niggas at OTB. Money from Oswego better show.

*Suddenly, rapid footfalls descending the stairs.* STARGYL *starts to bark.* SKRAM *enters in a whirlwind, a large paperboy bag slung over his shoulder. He is barely twenty, white, very thin, very pale. He has a very short crew cut. He wears a New York Knicks away jersey over a white T-shirt, absurdly long basketball shorts, and Timberland boots. There are crude tattoos about his arms.* STARGYL *stops barking.* SKRAM *runs to the window, jumps to grab the ledge, pulls himself up.*

SKRAM You chasin a ghost, G! (*siren*) Woo-woo-woo! Flatfooted faggits!

*He laughs, taps on the window, lets himself down.*

SKRAM  Got them jokers chasin they tails at the Jewel and shit.
Popsicles poppin out the box. Push-ups and Drumsticks rollin
down the aisles. TV dinners slidin everywhere. Security guards
breakin they ankles in the frozen food section. Pack my bag,
jump the turnstile, and I'm ghost, G.
   Jet down Jefferson. Catch a green light at six corners. Another
oh so friendly green on Black Road. I'm just a paperboy makin
my route, clockin my time. Shit, Count Chocula's gettin simpler
and simpler. Whaddup, yo?

*They tap fists, though* KITCHIN *is reluctant.* SKRAM *crosses to*
STARGYL *holds his fist out, greeting him.*

SKRAM  Star-gyl. Whaddup, G?

STARGYL *stares at his fist.*

SKRAM  Gimme a pound, yo!

STARGYL *stares at his fist, taps it.*

*From his bag,* SKRAM *removes two boxes of Count Chocula and a quart
of milk, sets them on a crate, crosses to the sink, grabs the plastic beach
pail, opens a box of cereal, pours its entirety into the pail, empties the
quart of milk into the pail, pulls a small plastic beach shovel out of the
back of his shorts, wolfs down the cereal.*

SKRAM  Hot as a motherfucker out there, G! Cars parked with
they windows open. People sittin in front of they cribs flappin

the newspaper. Lookin like they don't got no blood in they bodies. Tables. Chairs. Half the kitchen in the front yard. Niggas down by the river just standin in the mud. Standin all still like they waitin for somethin. It's like a hundred and twenty degrees out and shit.

KITCHIN  Where was you, B?

SKRAM  (*eating*) Where was I when, G?

KITCHIN  At seven motherfuckin thirty, that's when! I waited for you at the switch house for forty-five solid. Walkie-talkie nigga comes out askin me what I'm doin and shit. I'm holdin my fitty yesterdays like I'm tryin to sell the paper to the train tracks!

SKRAM  Aw, snap. My bad, Kitchin. I forgot.

KITCHIN  You forgot?

SKRAM  (*crossing to sink, cooling off, checking himself in the mirror*) I had other business.

KITCHIN  Other business.

SKRAM  Yeah, G. Other *bid*ness.

KITCHIN  Like what kind of *bid*ness.

SKRAM  Like *bid*ness of the other variety.

KITCHIN  You was chasin paste!

SKRAM  I wasn't chasin no paste, yo. I told you I stopped wif that nonsense.

KITCHIN  Man, you ain't stopped nothin.

KITCHIN *picks up a voided tube of glue off the floor, throws it at* SKRAM.

SKRAM  I'm tellin you I stopped, G. Shit started makin me dream funny. Dreamin bout sharks and whatnot. And they wasn't no regular-type TV sharks, yo. They was like sharks that can walk around and drive cars. Fuckin Calamityville Horror type joints. Chasin me down Gompers in sharkmobiles.

KITCHIN That shit don't do nothin but make you paranoid.

SKRAM Takes them hunger pains away.

KITCHIN That's why that nigga Blue Tip started duckin all the time. He always think someone be tryin to push him from behind. That's that pastehead paranoia. I'd rather *feel* my hunger. I'm starvin, I'm starvin. I don't need to pretend and shit.

SKRAM *moves to the entrance to the boiler room, presses his ear to the door.* KITCHIN *crosses to* STARGYL *with the pail of cereal and the shovel. He hands the pail to* STARGYL, *who lifts it to his face and drinks the rest.*

SKRAM Anyone come through?

KITCHIN I ain't hip. Just got back my damn self.

SKRAM Anybody come through, Stargyl? Any pigs and chickens?

STARGYL *shakes his head.*

SKRAM (*to* STARGYL) You shit your pants again? (*to* KITCHIN) He shit his pants again?

KITCHIN Naw, B.

SKRAM (*kicking* STARGYL'*s army men, they go flying*) I'm gonna have to scrape some fuckin Pampers for his intercontinental ass.

STARGYL *retrieves his army men, resets them.*

KITCHIN I said he didn't shit his pants, yo. And it's incontinent.

SKRAM Yeah, you know, right?

KITCHIN I do know. I ain't the one who can't read.

SKRAM  Condiments. Consonants. Condolences. It's all the same to me. (*to* STARGYL) Intercontinental bitch-ass nigga. (*crossing to* STARGYL) Why was he cryin?

KITCHIN  He wasn't cryin.

SKRAM  His face is wet!

KITCHIN  He just nervous and shit.

SKRAM  Nervous little punk.

KITCHIN  The light was going funny again.

SKRAM  Retarded crumbum sissy. Cryin at the light.

KITCHIN  Leave him be, yo. You know he gets amped about that simple shit.

SKRAM  Faggit! You wanna see my dick, bitch? (*taking his penis out*) Biggest dick in the world, G. You wanna touch it?

STARGYL *starts to cry.* SKRAM *laughs, stuffs his penis back in his pants.*

SKRAM  Put your sissy shoes on.

STARGYL *doesn't move.*

SKRAM  I said put em on, bitch!

STARGYL *removes his rotten sneakers and slips into the red pumps.*

SKRAM  Dance like a ho.

STARGYL *is frozen.*

SKRAM  Dance like a ho, nigga!

KITCHIN  C'mon, Skram. Stop with that shit, yo!

SKRAM  I want him to dance like the bitch he is, G. Look at him.

KITCHIN  Shit is mad unnecessary, B.

SKRAM  It ain't even your motherfuckin business, Kitchin. Dance, Stargyl!

STARGYL *pulls his pants up slightly revealing the pumps and his filthy ankles. He starts to dance very slowly, awkwardly.* SKRAM *claps a slow cadence.*

SKRAM  Go head on, ho. Do your sissy dance.

SKRAM *claps faster and faster.* STARGYL *crudely dances, trying to match the velocity of his claps.*

SKRAM  Woo-woo-woo!

KITCHIN *takes the pail back from* STARGYL, *crosses to the sink, rinses it out.*

SKRAM  Stop dancin.

STARGYL *bends down to remove the pumps.*

SKRAM  Did I say take em off?

STARGYL *stops.* KITCHIN *fills the beach pail with water and crosses to* STARGYL. *He takes his hand, puts it in the water, swirls it.*

KITCHIN  (*to* SKRAM) What the fuck is wrong with you, B?!

SKRAM  He *my* brother, G.

KITCHIN  Treatin him like a little bitch!

SKRAM (*indignant*) What?

KITCHIN What, *what*, nigga! That shit is like child abuse, yo!

SKRAM Stargyl knows I loves him.

SKRAM *crosses to* STARGYL, *fluffs his hair.*

SKRAM Star-*gyl*. Stargyl Super*star*. My nigga.

STARGYL *smiles.*

SKRAM See?

SKRAM *fake boxes him in the ribs.*

SKRAM Who's your nigga, Stargyl? Who's your nigga?

SKRAM *fluffs his hair again.*

KITCHIN He think we leavin him behind.

SKRAM We *should* leave his doofy-ass behind.

KITCHIN *takes the pail away, crosses to the sink, dumps the water.*
SKRAM *crosses to the entrance to the boiler room, presses his ear to the*
*door, pushes away, lies down.* STARGYL *continues to rearrange his*
*army men.*

SKRAM Money from Oswego call yet?

KITCHIN Payphone's broke, yo.

SKRAM No it ain't. You just gotta hit that bitch. Blue Tip called
me earlier. Joint was ringin loud and clear. Sounded like a ho
screamin for her pussy back. *Give it back, Skram! Give it back!*

KITCHIN  Nigga from Oswego still talkin two gees?

SKRAM  Shit, three. Maybe four he likes what he sees. Four gees, Kitchin. That's mad currency.

KITCHIN  I'm hip.

SKRAM  Mad, made-in-the-shade, drink-lemonade type bank.

KITCHIN  Yo, Fat Rick let me push the Electra today.

SKRAM  Word?

KITCHIN  Word is bond, B. Shit was mad lovely.


SKRAM *motions to* KITCHIN, KITCHIN *reaches into his shoeshine box, throws* SKRAM *a shoe brush.* SKRAM *brushes his Timberland boots.*


KITCHIN  Buck and a half and it's ours. Two bills and he throws in a new set of Michelins.

SKRAM  Finally get the fuck outta this heat. Away from this nowhere-ass town.

KITCHIN  Nowhere-ass, ho-infested, pastehead *tizzown.*

SKRAM  I'm tired of being one of these East Side river niggas that don't never get over the Hill. One day you twenty, the next thing you know you skeighty-eight and sportin the same burnt sneakers.

KITCHIN  Same old broke-ass kicks and shit.


*Again, outside, a broadcast public service announcement from the "Heat Relief" van.*


BROADCAST  ATTENTION, ATTENTION. THIS IS THE AGENCY FOR HEAT RELIEF. IT HAS BEEN BROUGHT TO OUR AWARENESS THAT THE FIRE HYDRANT ON THE CORNER OF JEFFERSON STREET AND GOMPERS BOULEVARD IS CONTAMINATED. UNIDENTIFIED

BACTERIA HAS BEEN DISCOVERED FROM THIS WATER SOURCE. DO NOT DRINK THE WATER FROM THE FIRE HYDRANT ON THE CORNER OF JEFFERSON STREET AND GOMPERS BOULEVARD. I REPEAT, DO NOT DRINK THE WATER FROM THE FIRE HYDRANT ON THE CORNER OF JEFFERSON STREET AND GOMPERS BOULEVARD.

SKRAM *crosses to the window, drops the shoe brush back in* KITCHIN's *box, pulls himself up to the window, peers out, lets himself down, crosses to the sink, falls down, gets back up, whirls.*

SKRAM  Why you pushin me?

KITCHIN  What?

SKRAM  You pushed me.

KITCHIN  I ain't even near you, nigga.

SKRAM  Why you pushin me, Stargyl?

KITCHIN  Nigga, please. He all the way over in the corner . . . Someone prolly been "pushin" you a *lot* lately.

SKRAM  Pushin me and callin me Larry. I think someone at the Jewel was whisperin that shit in my ear.

KITCHIN  I'm tellin you that's that paste fuckin with you, B.

SKRAM  Last nigga who called me Larry got a fork in his neck. (*turns to the door*) You feed her yet?

KITCHIN  *You* was sposed to feed her this mornin.

SKRAM  Aw, you didn't feed her, Kitchin?

KITCHIN  Feed her what, B? You keep eatin all the Count Chocula. Shit's sposed to be for her, yo. Fiendin-ass nigga.

SKRAM  I just brought two more boxes.

KITCHIN  You ain't *brought* shit. You scraped them joints.

SKRAM  Brought em, scraped em. What's the difference, G?

KITCHIN  Hooligan-ass bitch.

SKRAM  Suck on these nuts.

KITCHIN  Someday they gonna catch you, Skram. Throw you in the tank with the sharks and the troublefish. Have that ass bent over the foosball table.

SKRAM *crosses to the unopened box of Count Chocula, throws it to* KITCHIN. KITCHIN *catches it, throws it back to* SKRAM.

SKRAM  I said ain't feedin her.

KITCHIN  Sissy.

SKRAM  Thought you likeded feedin her.

KITCHIN  Thought light lit. Thought you farted but you shit.

SKRAM  The other day you said it was cool cuz it made you feel *hard*. You gotta feed her, yo.

KITCHIN  I don't *gotta* do shit!

SKRAM  She don't even look at me, Kitchin.

KITCHIN  That's cuz you be scarin her. Poppin off about "Who's your parents! Who's your parents!" Snappin matches at her.

SKRAM  Little-ass ho just sits there in the dark like that shit don't bother her. Ain't nuffin in her eyes. It's like starin into some bullet holes. And she don't even speak, yo. You feed her.

KITCHIN  I didn't like that shit last time, okay?

SKRAM  You didn't *like* it.

KITCHIN  Naw, B. Somethin about it wasn't right.

SKRAM  You goin soft, Kitchin? Spendin too much time wif that priestly nigga over at St. Jack's. Wipin off bingo cards. Readin the dictionary. What's his name—Father Feelgood and shit?

KITCHIN  Father *Freeman*, knucklehead.

SKRAM  Father Feelgood poppin that Jesus word. I saw you over there again today. Moppin the floor. Changin the holy water.

KITCHIN  Man, I was over there cuz they got them big church fans. All types of people was. Only place you can go to get out the heat, B.

SKRAM  Uh-huh.

KITCHIN  Nigga, all the air conditioners in the city is like mad busted!

SKRAM  Not the one at the Jewel.

KITCHIN  Well I wasn't over by there.

SKRAM  Or the one at the *car lot*. Fat Rick had that joint mad pumpin, Kitchin. Gave me goose pimplies and shit. Over at St. Jack's moppin the floor like a ho.

KITCHIN  Nigga, they be givin out free donuts at St. Jack's and you know it!

SKRAM  Pretty soon you'll be singin in the choir like a little bitch. Our Father who farts in heaven and shit. Father Feelgood'll be takin your temperature. Forcin his holy thermometer up your black ass . . . And what the fuck was doin on the train bridge?

KITCHIN  What?

SKRAM  I saw you up there.

KITCHIN  I was just lookin down at the water. Why the fuck you following me anyway?

SKRAM  Kitchin's going soft on us, Stargyl. When we get to New York I'm gonna have to find him some bitch panties. Some New York Knicks hotpants and shit.

KITCHIN  (*pointing to the boiler room*) This ain't *even* about bein soft, Skram. We shouldn'ta took her. We start off jukin quarters and stealin scratch tickets and now we fuckin kidnappin little kids!

SKRAM  All sweet and tender like a applesnap. My little black buttery applesnap. (*smooches the air*)

KITCHIN  Man, *fuck* you.

SKRAM  Maybe Stargyl'll feed her. (*to* STARGYL) You wanna feed her, Stargyl? Bitch-ass Kitchin's goin soft on us.

STARGYL *starts to cry.*

KITCHIN  See, now look whatchu gone and done.

SKRAM  (*to* STARGYL) You better eat that shit!

STARGYL *stops crying.*

SKRAM  Faggit-ass ho.

SKRAM *takes* STARGYL's *rings off his fingers, throws them across the room.*

KITCHIN  *You* go in there you so brave.

SKRAM  Choose for it.

KITCHIN  *Choose* for it?

SKRAM  Yeah, G. It's democratic and shit.

KITCHIN  And we a democracy, right?

SKRAM  Kitchin, Skram, and Stargyl, yo. Stars and Stripes forever.

KITCHIN  I got odds.

SKRAM  Odd motherfucker.

SKRAM AND KITCHIN  Once, twice, three, shoot.

*They both throw two fingers.* KITCHIN *loses.*

KITCHIN  Punk.

KITCHIN *takes the box of cereal, opens it, and pours the contents into the beach pail. A small plastic toy ring falls out. He picks it up off the floor, puts it in his pocket. He pours the carton of milk into the pail, sets the pail down, tears the new lost child photo off the back panel, stares at it for a moment, removes the bunch of pictures from his shorts, joins the new one with the others, returns the bunch to the inside of his shorts, retrieves the pail.*

SKRAM *crosses to* STARGYL, *reaches under his T-shirt, removes the shoelace key necklace, crosses to the entrance to the boiler room, inserts the key, unlocks the padlock, waves his hand at the door like a concierge.*

KITCHIN *grabs the flashlight from under the sink, slowly crosses to the entrance to the boiler room.*

KITCHIN  You got another spoon?

SKRAM *reaches into his shorts, removes another plastic beach shovel, drops it into the beach pail, opens the door.* KITCHIN *exits into the boiler room.* SKRAM *closes the door, sets the padlock in the hasp but does not lock it, then crosses to* STARGYL, *tucks the shoelace key necklace back under his shirt, crosses to the sink, cools off.* STARGYL *steps across his shrine of army men, retrieves one of the torn milk cartons. As he is retrieving the milk cartons,* SKRAM *flings water at him playfully.* STARGYL *crosses back to his corner, smiling, stands.*

SKRAM  Yo, Stargyl. Guess who I thought I saw today? You ain't *even* gonna believe me, Superstar. I'll give you one guess . . . Stand up straight, ho!

STARGYL *stands taller.*

SKRAM That's right. You guessed it: Mommy. Disco Jean. Disco Jean the Dancin Machine. Thought she was locked up and shit, right?

SKRAM *crosses to his paperboy bag, removes a fresh tube of airplane glue.*

SKRAM This bitch is walkin down the Hill, lookin like a fat-ass *dolphin.* Cracka her ass switchin in the breeze. Pussy stankin up the sidewalk. Drivin dogs under porches. Birds into barbecue pits. Her feet comin outta her stilettos. Fishnet stockins runnin everywhere. Breakin her ankles all the way down the Hill and shit. Disco Jean the Dancin Machine. Some old lopsided nigga from the bowlin alley trailin behind her all slow and careful. Panama hat. Big-ass collar flappin in the wind. Tryin to be slick like he ain't goin for some. Charlie Customer and shit. I'm like, *"Disco Jean! Disco Jean the Dancin Machine! Yo, Mommy!"*

She gets into a Lincoln Clown Car at the corner of Gompers and Jackson, right? Nigga wif the collar gets in after her. Takes his hat off before he opens the door like he a real gentleman and shit. They ride off down Jackson. Turn left on Truesdale. She prolly still lickin that nigga's butthole.

Thought for sure it was her but it wasn't. Crackhead ho.

SKRAM *unscrews the glue, snorts it into each nostril, crawls over to the staircase, takes his pants down, starts to masturbate on his knees, facing the shadows. He comes, takes a few deep breaths, rises, stomps out his mess into the floor, turns to STARGYL.*

ADAM RAPP

SKRAM  What?

SKRAM *moves to the heavy bag and starts to punch it violently. He counts out with each punch.* STARGYL *starts to cry.* SKRAM *reaches thirty-three, stops punching the heavy bag, paces around the room, catching his breath.*

SKRAM  Quit cryin, ho!

STARGYL *tries to stop crying.* SKRAM *pulls a lollipop out of the paperboy bag, removes the wrapper.*

SKRAM  Keep cryin and I ain't givin it to you. It's root beer, too, Pussy. (*holding out the lollipop*) Is this how you gonna be in New York City? If I get a job wif the Knicks how the fuck am I gonna get you hired if you can't act a like a man? They don't let sissies sell popcorn at Madison Square Garden, Stargyl.

STARGYL *stop crying.* SKRAM *hands him the lollipop.* STARGYL *puts it in his mouth.*

SKRAM  Good, right? Joint prolly melted and shit. So fuckin hot out.

SKRAM *paces, crosses to* STARGYL, *lifts his left pant leg, revealing a small snub-nosed .22 caliber revolver strapped to his calf.* SKRAM *removes the revolver, holds it up to the light, unlocks the chamber, spins the carriage, stops it, counts the bullets, pops the carriage back in, locks the chamber, spins it in his hand, aims at the heavy bag.*

SKRAM  What? . . . What?! . . . You late, motherfucka. I said you late! Blop, blop, blop!

*Faster*                                                                    129

SKRAM *holds his aim.*

SKRAM (*to the heavy bag*) Woo-woo-woo! Punk-ass nigga.

SKRAM *spins it in his hand again, then points it at* STARGYL.

*A knocking from the boiler room.* SKRAM *turns to it, startled, then laughs, crosses to* STARGYL, *re-sets the gun on his leg.*

KITCHIN Open the door, yo!

SKRAM *knocks back at* KITCHIN, *laughing. A momentary cacophony of knocking.* SKRAM *stops, opens the door.* KITCHIN *rushes out, falls to the floor, vomits into the floor drain.*

*Again, outside, a broadcast public service announcement from the "Heat Relief" van.*

BROADCAST ATTENTION, ATTENTION. THIS IS THE
AGENCY FOR HEAT RELIEF. PLEASE KEEP YOUR SMALL
CHILDREN OUT OF THE RIVER. I REPEAT, PLEASE KEEP
YOUR SMALL CHILDREN OUT OF THE RIVER.
KITCHIN She talked to me.
SKRAM She did?
KITCHIN I ain't lyin, B. Her voice is bug, yo.
SKRAM Bug like what?
KITCHIN Bug like that shit ain't even comin from inside her.
SKRAM Where's it comin from?
KITCHIN Somewhere else.

SKRAM *laughs, makes silly* Twilight Zone *sounds.*

KITCHIN  She told me she came from the river, Skram!

SKRAM  The *river*.

KITCHIN  She said she was borned in the belly of a fish.

SKRAM  Be serious, yo.

KITCHIN  That's what she said.

SKRAM  Who is she, fuckin Shark Girl or some shit?

KITCHIN  Think about it, Skram.

SKRAM  Think about what, Kitchin?

KITCHIN  You found her down by the casino boat.

SKRAM  So?

KITCHIN  (*removes the milk carton pictures from his shorts*) We ain't seen her on no milk carton. Or none of them posters on the telephone poles. She said some other bugged-out shit, too. Some biblical type shit.

SKRAM  (*teasing*) Some biblical, apocalyptical type nonsense?

KITCHIN  She told me that this big-ass storm is comin. That it's gonna rain so hard the river's gonna start flowin backwards.

SKRAM  Comin when?

KITCHIN  Tonight, B!

SKRAM  It ain't rained in mad weeks, G. The sidewalks on Gompers is like crackin from the heat. (*crosses to boiler room door*) Since when did that little ho start talkin?

KITCHIN  I ain't hip. I guess today.

SKRAM  So she like a weatherman?

KITCHIN  She somethin.

SKRAM  She a little *kid*, Kitchin!

KITCHIN  Skram, she told me the rain's gonna change to flies and that the flies is gonna change to fire!

SKRAM  Like *Indiana Jones and the Temple of Gloom* and whatnot.

KITCHIN  What if it's true?

SKRAM  That shit is *bananas*, yo!

*Faster*                                                                131

KITCHIN  She said the fish will protect us.

SKRAM  The *who*?

KITCHIN  The fish, B. The fish.

SKRAM  What fish?

KITCHIN  Fuck if I know!

SKRAM  Protect us from what?

KITCHIN  Prolly some seriously gloomy shit.

SKRAM  That sounds kinda dope, yo. Like some mad science fiction type nonsense. Stargyl, don't that sound dope?

KITCHIN  We should put her back, Skram.

SKRAM  Put her back! Put her back where, Kitchin—the supermarket? The fuckin shoppin mall?

KITCHIN  The river.

SKRAM  You seriously trippin, G.


*The sound of distant thunder. They stare up, then turn to each other.*


SKRAM  She do look kinda spooky, don't she?

KITCHIN  I'm hip, B.

SKRAM  All white and shit.

KITCHIN  Nowhere-ass lookin eyes.

SKRAM AND KITCHIN  Like she came from a fish, G/B.


*Again, distant thunder. They stare at each other a long moment, then* KITCHIN *starts for the stairs.*


SKRAM  Where you goin, Kitchin?


KITCHIN *exits up the stairs.* SKRAM *follows him halfway up.*


SKRAM  You comin back, right?!

ADAM RAPP

*No answer.* SKRAM *comes back down, paces a moment, falls to the floor, gets back up, whirls.*

SKRAM  Why you pushin me, Stargyl?!

STARGYL *takes a step back.* SKRAM *dusts himself off, looks around. Rolling thunder.* STARGYL *tries to swallow his hand.*

SKRAM  Get your hand out your mouth! Ain't nothin but a little thunder. Punk-ass nigga. *Should* leave you here.

STARGYL *takes his hand out of his mouth.*

SKRAM  Put your sissy shoes back on!

*The sound of a payphone ringing.* SKRAM *makes a dead sprint for the staircase, exits up the stairs. The payphone rings a few more times, then ceases.* STARGYL *stands very still in the corner.*

*Again, approaching thunder.*

*A knocking from within.* STARGYL *stares at the entrance to the boiler room.*

*More knocking.*

STARGYL *crosses to the entrance of the boiler room.*

*The light starts to flicker.* STARGYL *stares at it.*

*More knocking.*

*Faster*

STARGYL *turns to the door, reaches under his shirt, removes the shoelace key necklace. He inserts the key into the lock, unlocks it, removes the lock, quickly retreats to his corner, behind his plastic army. The light flickers. He turns and faces the corner.*

*The light stops flickering.*

*The boiler room door opens and a* GIRL *appears in the entrance, She might be six or seven. There is a small section of silver duct tape covering her mouth. On one hand, she wears a plastic toy ring, the prize from a Count Chocula cereal box.*

STARGYL *turns, stares at her curiously, crosses to her. She motions to him to go to his knees. He does so.*

*The* GIRL *removes the ring from her finger, places it on* STARGYL*'s pinkie. He stares at all his rings, smiles.*

*The* GIRL *reaches under her dress and removes a small fish, hands it to* STARGYL. *He holds the fish in his hand for a long moment, smiles.*

*He reaches into his back pocket, removes his comb, hands it to her. She takes the comb, runs it through her hair a few times, hands it back. He urges her to keep the comb. She runs the comb through his hair a few times, hands the comb back, he puts it back into his pocket. She holds her hand out as if to ask for something else.* STARGYL *reaches into his other pocket, removes the Zippo lighter, opens the top, flicks at it. She shakes her head, keeps her hand out.* STARGYL *returns the Zippo to his pocket, pulls up his pant leg, revealing the revolver. She nods.*

*He removes the revolver, hands it to her. She keeps it in his hand, turns*
*the nose toward her chest. He pulls the revolver back, shakes his head.*
*She pulls the nose of the gun toward her again, he pulls back again,*
*puts it back into the leg strap very quickly, slips the pant leg over the*
*gun.*

*She waves at him to bend down again. He does. She closes his eyes with*
*her fingertips. She removes the section of duct tape, sings.*

GIRL  (*singing*)
> *Florida orange juice on ice*
> *Sounds so nice*
> *In the morning*

> *Florida orange juice on ice*
> *Tastes so fresh*
> *The day is dawning*

> *Florida orange juice*
> *Healthy start*
> *To a brand new day*

> *Florida orange juice*
> *Vitamin C*
> *It's the sunshine way*

*She kisses both of his eyes, re-sets the duct tape back over her mouth, and*
*then turns and crosses to the boiler room. The door closes behind her.*

STARGYL *opens his eyes, stares at the fish in his hand.*

*The light begins flickering again.*

STARGYL *places the fish in his interior breast pocket, crosses to the boiler room entrance, re-padlocks the door, but doesn't lock it. He crosses to the corner, stands very still.*

*The light continues to flicker.*

*He crosses to the sink, grabs the plastic beach pail, runs the water, fills the pail, sets the pail in the center of the room, removes the fish from his interior breast pocket, stares at it in his hand for a moment, drops it into the pail, turns, crosses back to his corner, stands very still.*

*Footfalls descending the staircase.* KITCHIN *enters, He is holding a single donut wrapped in a napkin. He crosses to* STARGYL, *gives him the donut.*

KITCHIN  The Lord is my *shepherd*, I shall not want, Stargyl. That's that joint! The Lord is my shepherd, I shall not want. It's a Psalm, see?

*He removes a piece of torn paper from his shorts.*

KITCHIN  It's a Psalm of David. Psalm twenty-three and shit. (*reciting from the paper*) The Lord is my shepherd; I shall not want. He maketh me to lie down in green pastures; He leadeth me beside the still waters. Sounds like he on a motherfuckin golf course, don't it? He restoreth my soul; He guideth me in straight paths for His name's sake. Yea, though I walk through the valley of the shadow of death, I will fear no evil, for Thou art with me;

Thy rod and Thy staff, they comfort me. He must be sportin a gat or some shit.

Thou preparest a table before me in the presence of mine enemies; Thou hast a . . . *nointed* my head with oil; my cup runneth over. Surely goodness and mercy shall follow me all the days of my life; and I shall dwell in the house of the Lord for ever.

I don't even know what that shit means, yo, but Father Freeman said you just keep sayin that joint over and over.

*STARGYL nods, eats the donut.*

*The sound of violent rain.* KITCHIN *starts to pace around the room, reciting the prayer feverishly. He looks down, sees the beach pail, stops.*

KITCHIN What the fuck is that, yo? (*he bends down, jumps back*) Stargyl, you see that?

*STARGYL nods. Loud thunder.*

KITCHIN Where'd it come from, B?

*STARGYL shakes his head. A flash of lightning in the window.*
*STARGYL covers his eyes.* KITCHIN *continues to stare at the fish.*

*Descending footfalls.* SKRAM *enters in a sprint for the sink, vomits.*

SKRAM (*at sink*) Phone rang.
KITCHIN (*still staring into the bucket*) Cat from Oswego?
SKRAM Uh-huh.

KITCHIN  You talk to him?

SKRAM  Yeah, I talked to that nigga. Money's got a bug
voice, yo.

KITCHIN  Bug like what?

SKRAM  Bug like when he was talkin it was like it wasn't comin
through the phone.

KITCHIN  Where was it comin from?

SKRAM  It was like his voice was everywhere, G. Like that shit
was inside you.

KITCHIN  He on his way?

SKRAM  (*turning, facing* KITCHIN) Yeah, he on his way.

*The sound of thunder,* KITCHIN *turns to* SKRAM. *They look up at the
window.*

SKRAM  It's rainin sideways, yo. Like it's chasin you and shit.
Ain't never seen nothin like it, Kitchin. And the river . . .

KITCHIN  What about the river?

SKRAM  Shit is runnin backwards, G.

KITCHIN  Word?

SKRAM  Word is bond.

KITCHIN  Yo, Skram. This cat from Oswego. The dude with the
voice . . .

SKRAM  Uh-huh.

KITCHIN  He still talkin four gees?

SKRAM  Nigga's poppin some new shit.

KITCHIN  Yeah? What type of shit is that?

SKRAM  Like some genie-in-a-bottle type nonsense. He said we
could have whatever we want.

KITCHIN  Whatever we want.

SKRAM  As in anything there is.

KITCHIN  Damn.

SKRAM  I know. Damn. Nigga must got mad loot.

KITCHIN  Mad somethin . . .

*The light starts flickering,* KITCHIN *crosses to the bucket.*

SKRAM  What's in the pail?

KITCHIN  Huh?

SKRAM  The pail, G. You starin at it like it's talking to you and shit.

KITCHIN  You ain't even gonna believe me.

SKRAM  Why not?

KITCHIN  I think it's a shark, Skram.

SKRAM  A *shark*?

KITCHIN  A little baby shark. Shit is seriously bug, yo.

SKRAM  Do it got teef?

KITCHIN  Mad vampire type joints.

SKRAM *crosses to the beach pail, looks inside.*

SKRAM  This shit is bananas, Kitchin.

KITCHIN  I'm hip.

*Loud thunder.* SKRAM *sees that the padlock isn't closed, rushes to the door, locks it.*

KITCHIN  You straight, Stargyl?

STARGYL *nods.*

KITCHIN  You sure?

STARGYL *nods. A flash of lightning.*

KITCHIN  This shit is bug, right?

STARGYL *nods.*

KITCHIN  You still got your comb?

STARGYL *nods.*

KITCHIN  You wanna do your hair?

STARGYL *shakes his head.*

KITCHIN  You don't?

*The light starts to flicker again.*

KITCHIN  Stargyl . . . Stargyl Superstar.

*Again, outside, a broadcast public service announcement from the "Heat Relief" van.*

BROADCAST  ATTENTION, ATTENTION. THIS IS THE AGENCY FOR HEAT RELIEF. THERE IS A FLASH FLOOD WARNING IN EFFECT. HEAVY RAINS AND ELECTRICAL STORMS ARE IMMINENT! DO NOT GO OUTSIDE. I REPEAT, WHATEVER YOU DO, DO NOT GO OUTSIDE!

STARGYL *bends down and grabs two army men from his shrine. He crosses to* SKRAM *and* KITCHIN, *hands one to each, crosses back to his spot in the corner.* SKRAM *and* KITCHIN *stare at the army men.*

*The light is still flickering.* SKRAM *crosses to the light, taps it. It blows to total darkness. A flash of lightning.*

SKRAM'S VOICE  Oh, shit . . .

# ACT II

■　⬚　■　⬚

*Total darkness.*

*The sound of breathing.*

SKRAM'S VOICE  (*a whisper*) Kitchin . . .

*No response.*

SKRAM'S VOICE  (*a whisper*) Hey, Kitchin.

*No response.*

SKRAM'S VOICE  YO, KITCHIN!
KITCHIN'S VOICE  What, nigga?!
SKRAM'S VOICE  I was callin you, G!
KITCHIN'S VOICE  I heard you.
SKRAM'S VOICE  So answer then, bitch!
KITCHIN'S VOICE  (*swallowing*) My mouth was full.
SKRAM'S VOICE  Fulla what?
KITCHIN'S VOICE  I ain't hip. It tasted like a apple.
SKRAM'S VOICE  A *apple*!
KITCHIN'S VOICE  Yeah, nigga. A apple.
SKRAM'S VOICE  What apple?
KITCHIN'S VOICE  I ain't hip.
SKRAM'S VOICE  Can I get a bite?
KITCHIN'S VOICE  It ain't there no more.

*Faster*                                                    143

SKRAM'S VOICE  It ain't?

KITCHIN'S VOICE  That joint like disappeared, yo.

SKRAM'S VOICE  I feel like *I* fuckin disappeared.

KITCHIN'S VOICE  Yeah, me, too.

SKRAM'S VOICE  You floatin?

*No answer.*

SKRAM'S VOICE  Yo, Kitchin, you floatin?!

KITCHIN'S VOICE  Whatchu think, nigga?!

SKRAM'S VOICE  This shit is bug, right?

*No answer.*

SKRAM'S VOICE  It's bug right, Kitchin?

*No answer.*

SKRAM'S VOICE  Kitchin!

KITCHIN'S VOICE  Yeah, nigga, it's bug! It's fuckin bug!

*Pause.*

SKRAM'S VOICE  Yo, Kitchin, do the Electra got air-conditioning?
Cuz I'm hot as a motherfucker . . . Kitchin!

KITCHIN'S VOICE  *Shshshsh!*

*The sound of creaking in the staircase.*

KITCHIN'S VOICE  You hear that?

SKRAM'S VOICE  I hear it, G.

*The lighting of a match. A cigarette ember burns red.*

SKRAM'S VOICE  Yo, what the fuck is goin on?

*No response.*

SKRAM'S VOICE  Kitchin!
KITCHIN'S VOICE  Shut the fuck up, nigga!
SKRAM'S VOICE  Yo, Stargyl! . . . Kitchin, where's Stargyl?
KITCHIN'S VOICE  He over in the corner.
SKRAM'S VOICE  How do you know?
KITCHIN'S VOICE  Cuz I can smell the shit in his pants.
SKRAM'S VOICE  Stargyl, you shit your pants again?

*No response.*

SKRAM'S VOICE  Yo, Stargyl!

*No response.*

SKRAM'S VOICE  Bark if you can hear me, pussy!

*A single bark.*

SKRAM'S VOICE  Stargyl! Stargyl Superstar! . . . Yo, Kitchin, I'm so
hungry it feels like my stomach's maulin my back . . . I almost
ate a fuckin stick today. I was gonna put some mustard on it but I
thought about it and shit.

*Slowly, several candles are lit. As the room becomes illuminated, the
figures of* SKRAM *and* KITCHIN *can be seen dangling from the heavy*

bag chains. SKRAM is wearing the red pumps. Also, the figure of a MAN can be seen moving throughout the basement. He is eating an apple and smoking a cigarette. He is white, perhaps fiftyish, but ageless somehow. He wears a plain grayish suit. There is a wheelchair parked opposite SKRAM and KITCHIN, a metal suitcase placed next to the wheelchair.

SKRAM  Yo, who the fuck is that?!
KITCHIN  I ain't hip, B.

After the MAN finishes lighting all the candles, he takes a seat in the wheelchair and smokes and eats the apple. STARGYL has returned to his shrine of plastic army soldiers. He is now wearing SKRAM's Timberland boots and facing the corner. The back of his pants are soiled.

SKRAM  (to the MAN) Yo.

No response.

SKRAM  Yo, sir.

The MAN stares at SKRAM, tilts his head.

SKRAM  I think that nigga's deaf.

SKRAM suddenly performs a series of ridiculous hand gestures, an inane attempt at sign language. The MAN continues going about his business.

SKRAM  Maybe he retarded. (to the MAN) Yo, Money, you retarded? Like them niggas in the Tender Olympics.

ADAM RAPP

KITCHIN *Special* Olympics.

SKRAM Yeah, them doofy niggas wif the butts on they foreheads.

*The* MAN *smokes.*

KITCHIN (*to the* MAN) Scuse me.

*The* MAN *eats the apple.*

KITCHIN Um, sin . . . Yo, scuse me, sir. You the cat from Oswego?

SKRAM Yeah, G, you the cat from Oswego?

MAN Well, I don't know.

KITCHIN You don't know?

SKRAM Yeah, you don't fuckin know?

MAN Maybe *you* should tell *me.* Am I *the cat* from Oswego?

KITCHIN We askin *you.*

*The* MAN *smokes.*

KITCHIN Yo, we asked you a question.

SKRAM Yeah, we like asked you a question, Money!

MAN Did you? Is that what that was?

KITCHIN *and* SKRAM *stare at each other.*

KITCHIN Yo, sir, you got a name?

SKRAM Yeah, you got a fuckin name?!

MAN I don't know, do I?

KITCHIN We askin *you,* B.

SKRAM Yeah, we askin *you,* G!

MAN  Oh, I like this game.

KITCHIN  This ain't no game.

SKRAM  Yeah, G, this ain't no fuckin game!

MAN  A name game. I'm yellow, you're blue, let's walk together at the zoo. Maybe my name starts with a K. Or an S. Or maybe it's fun to guess . . . Maybe it's *Oz?*

KITCHIN  *Odds?*

SKRAM  As in one, three, five, seven, nine?

KITCHIN  Eleven, thirteen, fifteen, seventeen, nineteen.

SKRAM  You a odd motherfucker, G.

MAN  I'm impressed with your counting ability. But it's *Oz.* With a Z.

KITCHIN  Like Oswald and shit?

SKRAM  Yeah, like that nigga who shot George Washingmachine?

KITCHIN  It's Washing*ton.* And he shot *Kennedy,* knucklehead.

MAN  It's just Oz. Just oh so simply Oz.

KITCHIN  You don't got no last name?

SKRAM  Yeah, G, you don't got no last name?

MAN  As a matter of fact I *do* have a last name.

KITCHIN  Well what is it?

SKRAM  Yeah, G, what the fuck is it?

MAN  Maybe it's Wego?

KITCHIN  Wego.

SKRAM  As in Wego to the post office? Wego to the libary and shit?

MAN  Oz. Wego.

KITCHIN  Oswego.

SKRAM  Oswego.

MAN  You can call me Ozzie.

SKRAM  This shit is definitely bug, yo.

MAN  Or Mr. Wego.

KITCHIN  Cool.

SKRAM  Yeah, cool.

*The* MAN *smokes, exhales.*

MAN  So.

KITCHIN  So what?

SKRAM  Yeah, so the fuck what!?

*The* MAN *produces a bullhorn.*

MAN  (*into bullhorn*) What do you think of the rain?

SKRAM *and* KITCHIN *look at each other.*

MAN  (*into bullhorn*) Well?

SKRAM  Shit is mad hellefied.

MAN  Hellefied.

SKRAM  Yeah, G. Hellefied.

MAN  Hellefied is a good word. Do you know what it means?

SKRAM  Yeah, I know what that shit means.

MAN  Well, what does it mean?

SKRAM  Like you want a definition?

MAN  Sure.

SKRAM  Seriously?

MAN  (*into bullhorn*) Oh, I'm deliriously serious.

SKRAM  It means it's some crazy bugged-out shit's what it means.
Like it's chasin you and whatnot.

MAN  I would say that's part of it.

SKRAM  Like some mad, over-the-shoulder type nonsense.

MAN  (*pondering*) Mad, over-the-shoulder type nonsense.

*Faster*                                                        149

KITCHIN (*to* SKRAM) It means like Hell, knucklehead.

SKRAM That's basically what I said, G. Like Hell and shit.

MAN Hellefied rain. A rain of lost and slanted fire. It bleeds down through the soil and finds its passage into nefarious, boiling streams. A cleansing, whitehot rain.

SKRAM *and* KITCHIN *look at each other. The* MAN *smokes.*

SKRAM So Fozzie or Mr. Wingo or whatever your name is.

KITCHIN It's Ozzie, yo.

SKRAM Fozzie, Kamikaze, Kukla, Fran and Ollie.

KITCHIN Lemme talk to him, B.

SKRAM Then talk to him, nigga!

*The* MAN *smokes.*

KITCHIN Scuse me, Mr. Wego, sir. About you bein here and shit. Is we like doin business or what?

MAN Business?

SKRAM Yeah, G. *Bidness.*

KITCHIN Shut the fuck up, Skram!

MAN What kind of *bidness* exactly?

KITCHIN Makin deals. Clockin gees. That general businessy type shit people do.

MAN Oh, that. Yes, of course. You're talking about . . .

KITCHIN The girl, yo.

MAN The girl.

SKRAM Yeah, G, the fuckin girl!

KITCHIN We doin business, right?

MAN We are, yes. We are, in fact, in the midst of an all-

ADAM RAPP

important transaction. But first things first, it's better not to burst.

KITCHIN  Cool.

SKRAM  Yeah, G, cool.

*The* MAN *smokes.*

MAN  Cigarette?

KITCHIN  Naw, B.

*He offers one to* SKRAM.

SKRAM  Don't smoke squares, G. Hot enough in this motherfucker.

*The* MAN *smokes.*

KITCHIN  So what's first?

MAN  First?

KITCHIN  You said first things first.

SKRAM  Yeah, G. You said first things first!

MAN  Oh, of course, of course. Well, *first* I'd like to just say that I think those sissy shoes look sensational.

SKRAM *stares down at the pumps.*

SKRAM  Oh, shit!

MAN  (*to* SKRAM, *into bullhorn*) You show no gratitude.

KITCHIN  Say thank you, Skram.

SKRAM  What?

*Faster*

KITCHIN  Show some gratitude, yo.

SKRAM  Man, fuck you, Kitchin!

MAN  (*into bullhorn*) Not a good way to start off our *bidness* relationship.

KITCHIN  Just say it, B!

SKRAM  He tryin to punk me!

KITCHIN  So the fuck what! Just do it, nigga!


SKRAM *turns to the man.*


SKRAM  Thank you and shit.

MAN  You're welcome. They make me very glad. They make me want to do a glad dance. A glad dance gives everyone a chance. Have you ever done a glad dance before? It's loads of fun. Shimmy-shimmy cuckoo clock.

SKRAM  Yo, Kitchin, this nigga crazy.

MAN  I'm quite a dancer.

SKRAM  That's pretty bug, yo.

MAN  Bug?

SKRAM  Yeah, bug. Bug as in mad ridickilis.

MAN  Oh, I see—*ridickilis*. And why would my dancing be ridickilis?

SKRAM  Well, you can't be too good at it bein all locked down in that hospital chair. I mean, what the fuck is wrong wif you, G? You got like muscular catastrophe or some shit?

KITCHIN  Muscular *dystrophy*, B.

SKRAM  That joint got a motor?

KITCHIN  (*to* SKRAM) Knucklehead!

MAN  You'd be surprised at the amount of work I can get done in this chair.

SKRAM *revs an imaginary dirt bike.*

KITCHIN (*to* SKRAM) *Foolish*-ass nigga!
MAN If inspired I'm liable to lift right out of it.
SKRAM (*mocking*) Woooooooooooooooo!

*The* MAN *laughs, smokes.*

MAN (*to* KITCHIN) Can I ask you a question?
SKRAM (*laughing*) What, you wanna dance? Like we on a
telethon and shit?
MAN That's not what I had in mind. Not yet, anyway.
SKRAM So whatchu got in mind?
MAN Well, I was wondering if you were hungry. It doesn't
appear that you have much to eat around here.

KITCHIN *and* SKRAM *stare at each other.*

MAN (*into bullhorn*) Well, are you?
KITCHIN Yeah, B, we hungry.
MAN Are you starving? Are your stomachs *mauling your
backs?*
KITCHIN Yeah, B. We starvin. Starvin like Marvin.
MAN I was just wondering.
KITCHIN You wonderin?
MAN Yes. I spend a lot of time wondering. Wonder, wonder, call
upon the thunder. Add a pinch of fun and blow it all asunder . . .
So what do you say, boys, are you hungry?
KITCHIN Whatchu think, B?
SKRAM Yeah, G, whatchu think? You see any steaks fryin?

*Faster*                                                              153

MAN  I'll bet you think about food a lot. The smell of a good meal being prepared.

KITCHIN  Yeah, we think about food. We think about that shit all the time. Why, you givin out hot lunches?

MAN  No, unfortunately I'm not. But I was just *wondering* if one of you hungry fellas wouldn't mind eating a little fish.

KITCHIN  A little fish.

MAN  A small, insignificant fish. (*to* SKRAM) You like fish?

SKRAM  Yeah, G. I likes fish. Why, you got some fishsticks or some shit?

MAN  Maybe.

SKRAM  *Maybe.* What the fuck does that mean? You either *got* fishsticks or you *don't* got fishsticks.

KITCHIN  He talkin about the *fish* fish, yo.

SKRAM  What fish fish?

KITCHIN  The fish in the bucket, B!

MAN  (*to* SKRAM) If you eat that fish I'll give you everything in this suitcase.

KITCHIN  And whatchu got in that suitcase?

SKRAM  Yeah, G. Whatchu got in that suitcase, some mad crazy perverted type nonsense? Like four-by-four dildos and whatnot?

*The* MAN *opens the suitcase to reveal stacks and stacks of twenty-dollar bills.*

SKRAM  Oh, shit! Yo, G, you see that?

KITCHIN  I see it, B.

SKRAM  That's like crazy mad bank, yo. Later for that Electra. Fuck around and get a Benz and shit.

MAN  It's all yours.

SKRAM  Word?

MAN  As much as you want.

SKRAM  You hearin this, Kitchin?

KITCHIN  I'm hearin it, yo.

MAN  All you have to do is eat the fish.

SKRAM  Me?

MAN  Yes, you.

SKRAM  Why me?

MAN  Because I choose you, Larry. I think the fish would take to you. If you were a stream it would swim you supreme.

SKRAM  Yo, how did you know—

MAN  Oh, trust me, Larry, I know a lot of things.

SKRAM  So you want me to eat the fish.

MAN  I do, yes.

SKRAM  Like cook that joint up and shit?

MAN  I'd prefer it to be eaten raw.

SKRAM  Raw?

MAN  That is correct, my friend. It would mean more to me that way.

SKRAM  Like cut it up into little parts.

MAN  No. Whole.

SKRAM  The whole fish?

MAN  The fish in its entirety.

SKRAM  Like the fins and the teef and the eyeballs?

MAN  All of it, yes.

SKRAM  Like the insides and the butthole and all the boogies and shit?

MAN  It would be worth quite a sum.

SKRAM  (to KITCHIN) This shit is *bananas*, yo.


STARGYL *crosses to the beach pail, reaches inside, grabs the fish, puts it in his breast pocket, crosses back to his corner.*

*Faster*                                                                 155

SKRAM  Yo, Stargyl, what the fuck is you doin, G?

STARGYL *doesn't respond.*

SKRAM  Stargyl!
MAN  Looks like your friend has other plans.
SKRAM  Put that joint back, yo!

STARGYL *doesn't move.*

SKRAM  Put it back, nigga!

STARGYL *turns and faces the corner.*

SKRAM  Yo, let me down, Mr. Wiggles.
KITCHIN  Mr. *Wego.*
SKRAM  Let me down, Mr. Wego, so I can break that nigga's legs.
MAN  Oh, you can't do that.
SKRAM  Whatchu mean I can't do that?
MAN  Things are already set in motion.
SKRAM  You put us up here, didn't you?
MAN  In a manner of speaking, yes.
SKRAM  Stargyl, bring that motherfuckin fish back here, G!

STARGYL *doesn't move.*

SKRAM  Bring it back, punk-ass nigga!

STARGYL *doesn't move.*

SKRAM  Yo, let me down, Fozzie.

KITCHIN  Ozzie.

SKRAM  Ozzie, c'mon, yo!

MAN  I'll let you down.

SKRAM  You will?

MAN  Under one condition.

SKRAM  What condition?

MAN  That you dance with me.

SKRAM  Dance wif you?

MAN  That's correct.

SKRAM  Like *dance* dance?

MAN  Why, sure.

SKRAM  Like me and you like rumpshakin and shit.

MAN  Word is bond. A little do-si-do.


SKRAM *turns to* KITCHIN.


SKRAM  You hearin this, yo?

KITCHIN  I'm hearin it.

SKRAM  (*to the* MAN) I dance wif you and what?

MAN  I let you down.

SKRAM  You let me down.

MAN  So you can get the fish.

SKRAM  So I can get the fish.

MAN  So you can eat it.

SKRAM  So I can eat that joint.

MAN  So you can have the money.


SKRAM *turns to* KITCHIN.

SKRAM  So we can have the money.

KITCHIN  (*to the* MAN) What about the girl?

MAN  Oh, that's right, the girl.

KITCHIN  You still want her, right?

MAN  Yes. Yes, I do. I want her very much. But I'd really like to dance first.

SKRAM *turns to* KITCHIN.

SKRAM  I'm wif that.

MAN  You sure?

SKRAM  Hells yeah. Let me down. I'll dance wif you, G. But you better not try no crazy cumbum pervert shit cuz if I'm forced to I'll break your big ass down.

*The* MAN *wheels over to* SKRAM, *stands out of the wheelchair, reaches up, effortlessly removes* SKRAM *from the chain, lets him down.* SKRAM *stands awkwardly facing him for a moment.*

MAN  Perhaps your friend could sing us a little glad song.

SKRAM *turns to* KITCHIN.

SKRAM  Sing us a song, G.

MAN  Something with a little life in it.

KITCHIN *starts to hum a slow spiritual. The* MAN *holds his hand out to* SKRAM.

MAN  Shall we?

SKRAM *takes his hand. The* MAN *pulls him close. They slow dance to the spiritual,* SKRAM *still wearing the red pumps. As the song progresses, they draw closer and closer.*

KITCHIN  *(singing)*
>*Florida orange juice on ice*
>*Sounds so nice*
>*In the morning*
>
>*Florida orange juice on ice*
>*Tastes so fresh*
>*The day is dawning*
>
>*Florida orange juice*
>*Healthy start*
>*To a brand new day*
>
>*Florida orange juice*
>*Vitamin C*
>*It's the sunshine way*

KITCHIN *continues to hum while the* MAN *and* SKRAM *continue to dance, slower and slower, until they come to a very dead rest. The* MAN *continues to hold* SKRAM *warmly, staring intently into his eyes.*

*The sound of rain. The sound of thunder.*

MAN  Now go get the fish.

SKRAM *nods. He crosses to* STARGYL, *who is still turned toward the corner.* SKRAM *turns* STARGYL *around.* STARGYL *clutches his breast* pocket. SKRAM *attempts to pry his hands away.* STARGYL *falls to the floor, still clutching his breast pocket.* SKRAM *strikes him across the face, pries his hands away, thrusts his hands into* STARGYL*'s interior breast pocket, steals the fish, crosses back to the* MAN, *turns to* KITCHIN.

SKRAM  Yo, you want some of this, G?

KITCHIN *shakes his head.* SKRAM *turns to the* MAN. *The* MAN *makes a gesture to the suitcase full of money, nods.* SKRAM *raises the fish above his head, lowers it slowly to his lips, swallows the fish whole.*

*The* MAN *moves to* SKRAM, *embraces him tenderly for a moment, then guides him to one of the crates, seats him.*

*Suddenly, the sound of insects buzzing.* SKRAM *turns to* KITCHIN.

SKRAM  You hear that, Kitchin?

KITCHIN *nods. The buzzing swells for a moment.*

SKRAM  Yo, what is that, G?

*The* MAN *wheels over to the window, peers up.*

MAN  It's the flies.
SKRAM  The flies?
MAN  The din of the rainfly. Such a pretty sound.

SKRAM *and* KITCHIN *stare at each other, baffled.*

SKRAM  So, Mr. Wego.

MAN  Yes, my little friend.

SKRAM  About the girl . . .

MAN  The girl. Of course, the girl.

KITCHIN  We should put her back, Skram! Fuck all this nonsense!

MAN  Oh, you don't want to do that.

KITCHIN  We should do it, Skram!

MAN  But it's too late. Things are already set in motion.

KITCHIN  What things?

MAN  Well, the things that matter most, friend. Hasn't anything ever mattered to you? Haven't you always wanted to get on with your life? Get out of this *nowhere-ass ho-infested tizzown*? Think about that.

KITCHIN  Whatchu gonna do with her?

MAN  What am I gonna do with her? There's so much really. So much *to* do. I could show you if you'd like. Would you like me to show you?

*KITCHIN nods. The MAN crosses to KITCHIN, who is still attached to his hook.*

MAN  I'm going to open my mouth. I'm going to open it as wide as I can. Wider than anything you've ever seen. And when I do, I want you to look inside. Simply look inside and note what you see. What you see is what will be done to her. Now don't close your eyes or you'll miss the surprise.

*KITCHIN nods. The MAN opens his mouth wide. KITCHIN peers inside. A look of terror grows in his face. He starts to scream. After a moment, the MAN closes his mouth.*

MAN  You see?

KITCHIN *nods. He is hysterical.*

MAN  (*to* SKRAM) I think your friend needs some air. (*to* KITCHIN) Would you like some air?

KITCHIN *nods desperately.*

*The* MAN *crosses to* KITCHIN, *frees him from the heavy bag chain, sets him down. The* MAN *takes* KITCHIN*'s face in his hands, forces his mouth open, starts to blow into* KITCHIN*'s mouth.* KITCHIN *pushes himself away, falls down, quickly gets to his feet, and then makes a dead sprint for the staircase, scrambles up the stairs, exits. Over the following, the* MAN *starts to move from candle to candle, blowing each one out.*

MAN  So, looks like my business is done.
SKRAM  What about the girl?
MAN  What about her?
SKRAM  Don't you want her and shit?
MAN  I do, son. I do want her.
SKRAM  But you ain't gonna take her wif you?
MAN  No. As a matter of fact, I'm not. Actually, I'm *not* going to take her with me.
SKRAM  Why not?
MAN  Why not?
SKRAM  Yeah, G, why the fuck not? You came all this way. Oswego's like a forty-five-minute drive and shit.
MAN  Oh, I don't drive. I fly. Everywhere. Over the hills. Over the dells. Over the firelight. I rarely use my legs. That's why I have

such a hard time walking. My work is done. She's all yours
now.

SKRAM  I don't want that little ho.

MAN  Oh, but I think you do.

SKRAM  What the fuck am I sposed to do wif her?

*After the* MAN *finishes blowing out the last candle, he starts to leave.*
*Just as he reaches the foot of the stairs:*

SKRAM  Yo, I don't want her, Ozzie!

*The* MAN *stops, turns.*

MAN  *Once long ago there was a boy named Larry.*
*Not Johnny or Dellwood or Gerald or Gary.*
*He was bright as the sky and shiny as tin.*
*He had a mother so fat, and a brother so thin.*

*They lived in a house on Blueberry Lane.*
*A house made of bread and old candycane.*

*Mother was sad, her face long as the Nile.*
*It showed in her eyes and her upside-down smile.*

*She was hungry as mice but there was nothing to eat.*
*Not a speck in the fridge, not a crumb on the street.*

*Then one day she started eating the walls!*
*After all they were bread,*
*not stone nor brick stalls.*
*She thought, The wall in the kitchen*

*might taste pretty good.*
*It might be delicious! I should eat it, I should!*

*So she ate through the wall, she made a big hole.*
*She had to act fast, the boys couldn't know.*
*She looked through the hole and what did she see?*
*People to know and places to be!*

*She could fly to Japan or sail in a boat!*
*She could jump in the sea and just simply float!*
*She could go catch a bird or climb a tall tree!*
*There were horses and spaceships and magic TV!*

*That night while the boys were sleeping and dreaming*
*she jumped through the wall and ran away screaming.*
*Beyond the Old Sea. Past the last train.*
*Far from their house on Blueberry Lane.*

*When Larry awakened he searched for their mother.*
*It was high time to feed his big baby brother.*
*She wasn't here. She wasn't there.*
*She wasn't up or down.*
*Mommy!, Larry called, but Mommy couldn't be found.*

*A month went by. And then two more.*
*And then another—that made four!*

*It was scary*
*but Larry was brave as a bear.*
*But the food was all gone, they couldn't eat air.*

*So just like their mother,*
*they began eating the house.*
*They nibbled it raw with the speed of a mouse.*
*Walls made of bread—still a couple of those.*
*One by the sink and one by the stove.*

*But after a while there was nothing but holes.*
*Nothing but holes for the wind and the crows.*

*So they left their old place on Blueberry Lane.*
*They walked to the railroad and counted the trains.*

*They washed in the river, slept under trees,*
*ate beetles and snowballs and old dirty leaves.*

*The* MAN *hands a tube of glue to* SKRAM, *gently seats him in the wheelchair.*

MAN   *One day in June they saw a woman walk by.*
        *Did she look familiar! Familiar, oh my!*
        *She was fat as a whale and, my, did she wiggle!*
        *She waddled so fast, her whole body jiggled.*

        Momma! *Larry screamed.* It's Mommy! It's Mother!
        She's come back to get us, Big Baby Brother!

        *Larry knelt down and prayed at her feet.*
        Mommy, oh Mommy. Dear Mommy My Sweet.
        Where did you go?! We've had nothing to eat.

*He hugged her and squeezed her, and tickled her nose.*
*He kissed her fat, all ten of her toes.*
*But Mommy was hungry, she had nothing for Larry.*
*She kicked him, slapped him, and goddamn it was scary.*

*Poor little Larry lay heaped in the road.*
*And his miserable heart shrank small as a toad.*
*Big Baby Brother couldn't utter a sound:*
*his tongue had gone still as a stump in the ground.*
*Mommy!, he tried, but nothing was said.*
*And since that sad day, his poor voice was dead.*

SKRAM *starts to cry.*

MAN   *Away Mother walked, fat as a hog.*
*Big Baby Brother lay long as a log.*
*It was getting so late, there was nowhere to go.*
*There would be rain and cold wind and blizzards of snow.*

*Their stomachs would howl*
*and where would they sleep?*
*It was a sad little time.*
*Too sad to weep.*

The MAN *embraces* SKRAM *tenderly.* SKRAM *continues crying.*

The MAN *takes* SKRAM's *face in his hands and kisses his mouth for a
long moment. They both keep their eyes open. It is a transaction more
than anything sexual.*

MAN  Go to her, my little friend. Simply go to her. You'll know what to do.

*The MAN crosses to his things, slowly gathers his wheelchair, folds it, leaves the suitcase full of money. He ascends the stairs with his wheelchair, exits.*

SKRAM *takes off the pumps, sprints halfway up the stairs, looks, runs back down the stairs, sprints to the window, peers out, jumps down, then starts to pace around the room. His pacing gains velocity, like that of a wild animal trapped in a cage. After a moment he crosses to* STARGYL, *stands over him for a moment, drags him out from behind his shrine of plastic army men.* STARGYL *attempts to get away.* SKRAM *kicks him in the face, then starts to beat him on the floor. It ends with* SKRAM *kicking* STARGYL *in the ribs.* STARGYL *is crouched in the center of the basement, his hands shielding his head.* SKRAM *reaches under* STARGYL's *shirt and removes the shoelace necklace with the key, then the revolver from his leg.* SKRAM *crosses to the entrance to the boiler room, inserts the key, turns it, removes the lock. He opens the door, stands in the entrance for a long moment. He then unscrews the top to the glue, snorts it, staggers a bit, drops the tube of glue, enters the boiler room, leaving the door open.*

*The sound of loud thunder.*

*The sound of flies buzzing.*

*Two gunshots.*

*The faint sound of fire crackling.*

*Faster*

STARGYL *slowly rises off the floor, crosses back to his corner, stands. The sound of the flies buzzing grows louder. Slow footfalls can be heard descending the stairs. Moments later,* KITCHIN *appears. He is drenched from the rain and there are ruptured flies all over his football jersey. He is holding a large, white offertory candle, a small flame burning at the top. He stands very still for a moment.*

KITCHIN The flies is everywhere, Stargyl. Like pepper falling from the sky. Buzzin all in your mouth. Your eyes. The holes in your nose.

I run over to St. Jack's. Run like there's rain burnin through my blood. Never run so fast in my life. My legs is just goin wild. Think if I run fast enough it'll make that wind leave my stomach. Make them cats stop cryin.

I get to St. Jack's and everyone's gone. No priest. Nobody in the pews. Not even no birds swoopin down. Thought niggas might be standin in fronta the fans. Thought the flies woulda drove folks inside. But it was mad empty, yo. The way shit is empty when all you can hear is the sound of your own blood movin through you. The blue Jesus just starin back at you like he hungry.

So I scream. I'm like, "Where's everybody at?!" I'm like, "Yo, God! Yo, God, where is you, G?!" But there ain't no answer. Only the sound of them flies buzzin. So I grab a candle. Big white one right off the altar. And I set St. Jack's on fire, Stargyl. The cross. The pews. All the pictures. Fire burns up the walls like little hands runnin. Windows pop. Flames shoot right through the roof.

Thought God would see it. Hear them windows poppin. See them birds burnin. Somethin. But God didn't hear nothin, Stargyl. Like that shit didn't even happen. It's like that nigga's asleep.

*The faint sound of fire crackling.*

SKRAM *appears in the entrance to the boiler room, holding the revolver. His eyes are huge, ghostly.*

SKRAM  Hey, Kitchin . . . You ready to break north and shit?

*No response.*

SKRAM  Let's go, yo. Get the fuck outta here. Just you and me, G.

SKRAM *points to* STARGYL.

SKRAM  Leave that nigga here.

KITCHIN *doesn't move.*

SKRAM  C'mon, Kitchin.

KITCHIN *doesn't move.*

SKRAM  What's up, G?

KITCHIN *doesn't move.*

SKRAM  You ain't comin?

KITCHIN *shakes his head.*

SKRAM  You ain't?

*Faster*                                                    169

KITCHIN *shakes his head.*

SKRAM  Yo, you know that shit Ozzie showed you. That shit that was in his mouth?

KITCHIN *nods.*

SKRAM  Well, I got it now. See?

SKRAM *opens his mouth very wide and shows* KITCHIN. KITCHIN *is filled with sorrow.* SKRAM *closes his mouth.*

SKRAM  Pretty dope, right? You want some?

KITCHIN *shakes his head.*

SKRAM  You sure?

*No response.*

SKRAM  Punk-ass nigga.

SKRAM *crosses to* STARGYL, *pulls his Timberland boots off of* STARGYL's *feet, puts them back on, crosses to the suitcase, closes it, grabs the handle.* SKRAM *crosses to the staircase, ascends the stairs slowly.* SKRAM *stops, turns to* STARGYL.

SKRAM  Yo, Stargyl, you see Mommy tell her I said she a ho.

SKRAM *exits up the stairs with the suitcase. The light starts to flicker.* STARGYL *crosses to the center of the room with the milk carton boat,*

*sets it down, then crosses the entrance to the boiler room, exits.*
KITCHIN *crosses to the center of the room, sets the offertory candle*
*down, kneels beside it.*

STARGYL *re-enters with a life-sized little girl doll cradled in his arms.*
*She is dressed identically to the* GIRL *who visited* STARGYL *toward the*
*end of Act I. Her eyes have been shot out.* STARGYL *sets her in the milk*
*carton on the floor.* KITCHIN *starts to weep.* STARGYL *grabs the beach*
*pail, places* KITCHIN's *hand in the water.*

STARGYL  *(singing)*
>       *Florida orange juice on ice*
>       *Sounds so nice*
>       *In the morning*
>
>       *Florida orange juice on ice*
>       *Tastes so fresh*
>       *The day is dawning*
>
>       *Florida orange juice*
>       *Healthy start*
>       *To a brand new day*
>
>       *Florida orange juice*
>       *Vitamin C*
>       *It's the sunshine way*

*Lights fade as* STARGYL *swirls the water around* KITCHIN's *hand. The*
*sound of fire can be heard crackling in the streets.*

# FINER

# NOBLE

# GASES

■  ▓  ■  ▓

# AUTHOR'S NOTE

Early in a playwright's career, if you're lucky, a new work gets a reading or two, and then, without the fortune of a production somewhere, it often winds up under your bed or among drifts of other perished manuscripts. I wrote the first draft of *Finer Noble Gases* during the winter of 1999, while I was recovering from a severely herniated disc. Bedridden and reliant on painkillers, I kept falling asleep and waking up with my hands on the keyboard; eventually, I wound up with this weirdly structured play about a failed rock band called Less. The plot was too fuzzed-out from narcotics to make much sense, and, when my doctor refused to write me another prescription, the process of honing it became at best even hazier—knitted together as it was by dreams, the occasional, half-remembered shadowy visit from a friend, and what felt like entire seasons of back pain.

After I got on my feet I brought the play into my class at Juilliard, where a few of the Group 28 actors read it for me. It was probably my first lucid experience with the story. Since then, providence has afforded me several cracks at *Finer Noble Gases*. It started with Chris Fields, who directed a staged reading of it at the Ojai Playwrights Conference in the summer of 1999. Chris and his actors did a terrific job and my experience in Ojai gave me faith that I had something that could hold an audience. A few weeks later, Carolyn Cantor, who had received a directing grant from the Williamstown Theater Festival, mounted a kind of guerrilla workshop production in a log cabin. It was fully (though minimally) realized, with lights and sets and costumes, but it wasn't being offered to the general public. The audience consisted largely of the Williamstown non–Equity company members and

*Finer Noble Gases*

other festival stragglers. David Korins, who designs a lot of my work now, literally pirated the walls from another Williamstown production that had closed. The actors worked for free and I don't think there was even a stage manager involved. Carolyn rehearsed with the actors for a little less than three weeks and I joined them for the final four days. The play was performed only twice, for a late-night audience, who mostly sat on the floor of the cabin. Despite the makeshift production, things went well and I left Williamstown encouraged that *Finer* would find an audience with a proper run. But after a seemingly strong start, several theaters passed on it and I was left dejected and second-guessing the play. I thought that, despite its comic energy, it was too dark, that it was tonally confused, that perhaps *I* was confused. I put the most recent draft in a box in my closet and started work on a novel.

Several months later, feeling sentimental, I pulled it out of that box in my closet. Rereading the play opened a door for me: I had been writing a lot of music at the time, often a song a day on my guitar; I wanted to somehow impart to the work what this band the play centered around might have been when they were at their best, so I did some rewriting, brought the band element more to the foreground, and submitted it to the 2001 O'Neill Playwrights Conference, where it was accepted (thank you, Jim Houghton). With Carolyn Cantor again at the helm and guiding it beautifully through another week of rehearsals, I started to understand how to theatricalize the rock band element. In the previous versions of the play, the group's prowess as musicians was merely hinted at. I thought putting it onstage in a kind of "dream of what was" would be exciting for an audience, especially following the long, sustained scenes of spare dialogue and physical inertia.

At the 2002 Humana Festival, Michael Garcés encouraged me

to take the band element even further. For the O'Neill production, we had to suggest the rock anthem that punctuates the final scene, with the actors playing air guitars and miming drums, etc. When Michael and I discussed casting, it became apparent we both believed it was essential that Less be a legitimately talented band that could really perform with the power and conviction needed. So we hired actors who also happened to be terrific rock musicians. I already knew two: Dallas Roberts, who was cast as Chase, is an excellent guitarist, and Michael Chernus, who played Lynch, is a multimusician and an accomplished bassist. Rob Beitzel, the Less front man, was cast as Staples, and thanks to the amazing drummer Ray Rizzo, who happened to be a local Louisville rock legend, the fourth member of the band, Speed, emerged. (Speed didn't exist in earlier drafts and he sort of willed himself into the play when I realized how essential a good drummer is. At the time I had been playing music mostly by myself, alone in my room, and had only recently begun playing with a drummer, which was an enormous eye-opener.) Each day, after five hours of play rehearsal, we would rehearse another three as a band. Dallas, Rob, Michael, and Ray brought Less to life in ways that I had never imagined. The band played legitimate gigs at local Louisville clubs and developed something of a cult following. It was very exciting for me to see rock 'n' roll fans coming to the theater.

After the Louisville production, I started thinking a lot about these men, how the tragedy of the early thirties was not so much about what they hadn't accomplished than about how they'd lost the will to stay connected to their art, and ultimately to one another. With this, the character of Dot—an eleven-year-old girl from Seattle, who used to enter the play near the very end—by comparison started to feel overly symbolic to me. I have to admit in the beginning I thought I was being clever by having this child, who clearly represented the Information Age, appear and start cleaning up the band's apartment. At Louisville, while the young actress who played her did a great job, I could feel my own figurative hand pressing down way too hard on the play, and the organic hyper-realism that had been developed during rehearsal suddenly felt compromised by this character who referred to herself and her parents by their e-mail addresses. Over time, her role morphed into that of a young boy named Pete, whom Lynch finds frozen to death in Tompkins Square Park—a radical transformation, to say the least. Other than the child functioning as a cipher for the obvious themes of men behaving like boys and the terror of artistic and spiritual paralysis, my only explanation for Pete replacing Dot is that he, although dead, feels somehow more real to me than Dot ever did. In the end, a boy so lost he's ceased living, who emerges out of the world of this play that deals with arrested men who have forgotten how to feel, is more authentic to me than a girl from Seattle who spends her time on stage tidying a room and talking about the beauty of technology. I see Pete abandoned in the park, sitting on a bench, wearing Rollerblades, his hands freezing but still making animal masks, wearing a too-thin coat, his parents back in their apartment in Brooklyn or Queens or the Upper West Side, knowing all too well what the cold might do to the child they've left behind.

The great master Chekhov said, "Kill your darlings." I'd like to believe that I have perhaps made my play better by trading in one live darling for a deceased one. This is a recurring motif for me, but I can't say for certain why I keep populating my plays with these troubled, sometimes lifeless children. A few years ago, I saw a picture of U.S. embassy soldiers roasting a local Somalian child over a flaming oil drum. The picture still haunts me and I am of

ADAM RAPP

the mind that we write about what keeps us up at night, and these are the kinds of things that prevent me from sleeping. With *Finer Noble Gases*, it was important that the only items that are brought into the apartment from the outside world are a pair of McDonald's Happy Meals, a bloody knife, and the frozen corpse of a boy. Although we are believed to be a great nation, we are in many ways a cold, unfeeling, consumption-obsessed country whose machinery often produces innocent casualties. Kids kill other kids for basketball shoes. Junior high schools are outfitted with metal detectors. Children are abandoned in the parking lots of supermarkets. Modern pharmaceuticals are the subject of lengthy television commercials. The winters keep getting colder.

There are rare moments when you are lucky enough to discover new truths about your work. With this play, as it has slowly shifted, evolved, and continued to reveal itself to me, I have finally learned that while it is largely about a band of emotionally disconnected men, perhaps its most important thread is that despite the numbing-out that can happen during several months in front of a television, despite a season or two of bad weather and the effects of an increasingly user-friendly, technologically centered, sometimes violent, ineffectual culture that can make us feel like staying inside for the rest of our lives, we can still somehow wrest ourselves from these prophylactic moorings, get off the sofa, and move again, whether it be across the living room, out the front door, or toward the embrace of another.

I feel incredibly fortunate that *Finer Noble Gases* has had so many lives. Five years from its original inception, it has finally found its way back to New York, where it was born in a dingy East Village apartment on East 10th Street.

This play would not have evolved if it wasn't for the dedicated commitment of more than thirty actors and all of those wonderful directors whom I have named above. I would also like to thank Marc Masterson of the Actors Theater of Louisville and David Van Asselt of the Rattlestick Playwrights Theater.

—NEW YORK CITY, 2004

ADAM RAPP

*Finer Noble Gases* was originally workshopped in Waterford, Connecticut, at the O'Neill Playwrights Conference in 2001 (Jim Houghton, Artistic Director). It was directed by Carolyn Cantor. The cast was as follows:

| | |
|---|---|
| STAPLES | *Robert Beitzel* |
| CHASE | *Michael Chernus* |
| LYNCH | *Marc Lynn* |
| GRAY | *Connor Barrett* |
| DOT | *Nicole Pasquale* |

*Finer Noble Gases* was subsequently produced in Louisville, Kentucky, at the Humana Festival of New American Plays in March 2002. It was directed by Michael John Garcés; sets were designed by Paul Owen; costumes by Christal Weatherly; lights by Tony Penna; and sound by Vincent Olivieri. The production stage manager was Charles M. Turner III. The cast was as follows:

| | |
|---|---|
| STAPLES | *Robert Beitzel* |
| CHASE | *Dallas Roberts* |
| LYNCH | *Michael Shannon* |
| SPEED | *Ray Rizzo* |
| GRAY | *Jeffery Bean* |
| DOT | *Alaina Mills* |

*Finer Noble Gases* had its New York premiere in the fall of 2004 in a production by the Rattlestick Theater Company (David Van Asselt, Artistic Director) at the Rattlestick Theater. It was directed by Michael John Garcés; sets were designed by Van Santvoord; costumes by Elizabeth Hope Clancy; lights by Jane Cox; and sound by Eric Shim. The cast was as follows:

| | |
|---|---|
| STAPLES | *Robert Beitzel* |
| CHASE | *Dallas Roberts/Patrick Derragh* |
| LYNCH | *Michael Chernus* |
| SPEED | *Ray Rizzo* |
| GRAY | *Conor Barrett* |

# CHARACTERS

STAPLES        *thirtyish, a spaceman with a very low pulse*

CHASE          *thirtyish, lazy, a charmer*

LYNCH          *thirtyish, larger than the others, terrified, terrifying*

SPEED          *thirtyish, comatose, a good drummer*

GRAY           *thirtyish, a lonely eccentric*

YOUNG BOY   *six, deceased*

# SETTING

An East Village apartment near Tompkins Square Park in New York City. Winter.

*A filthy East Village apartment near Tompkins Square Park. A typical pre-war Skinner box. A naked window leading to a fire escape. A neon beer sign, turned off. A half-collapsed, stained, and bucket-seated sofa, duct tape over the cushions. A coffee table with three glass bowls of pills: a bowl of blue pills; a bowl of pink pills; a bowl of yellow pills. The bowls are nearly arranged, perfectly spaced. A random, street-plucked chair. An equally random ottoman. A full drum set, a microphone stand and mic next to the drum set. An electric and a bass guitar propped on guitar stands. A bass amp. A guitar amp. A keyboard set up on a stand, an amp next to it. A few microphone stands set up with mics. Some random cords and wires snaking indecipherably. Sweat socks, junk mail, crumpled beer cans, old set lists, pizza boxes, pools of things here and there. Drifts of debris. A wall of McDonald's Happy Meal boxes. A hallway leading to unseen bedrooms. A front door. A small TV surveillance monitor housed in the wall next to the door. Underneath the monitor, someone has scrawled "MIKE" in black indelible ink. There are several shoulder-height holes in the wall. A kitchen sink choked with dirty dishes. A filthy table with scattered chairs. A trash can painted like R2D2.*

*CHASE and STAPLES, thirtyish, are sitting on the sofa, watching TV. They wear wrinkled thrift-store clothes. They are fully bearded and they smell. There is the feeling that the two of them have been living on the sofa since the previous spring. STAPLES sits very still. CHASE fidgets a bit, his feet never touching the floor.*

*Next to the chair, ANOTHER MAN lies on the floor. He is neither sleeping nor thinking. He is thirtyish, bearded, and lives in his underwear.*

*Finer Noble Gases*

*The only source of light is the blue throb of the TV and a yellowish glow from the back of the apartment where lights have been left on. The noise of the TV should play throughout, but barely audible; an animal being tortured.*

STAPLES  I had this dream last night that I was a robot. Big metal robot. I was crying but nothing was coming out. I could feel the crying. In my throat. But no tears. And I didn't have any balls. Instead I had a light switch. I kept trying to turn it on but all it did was make this buzzing noise.

CHASE *puts his hand down his pants.*

CHASE  Wow.
STAPLES  I know, right?

*They watch.*

CHASE  You do the blues or the pinks?
STAPLES  The blues.
CHASE  The pinks are good. You shouldn't do more than two. Never do more than two. I think some guy did four once.
STAPLES  Whoa.
CHASE  I know, right?
STAPLES  Halfs or fulls?
CHASE  Fulls.
STAPLES  What happened to him?
CHASE  He got on a bus. The M-Fifteen, I think. Tied the driver to a pole and drove through yellow lights all the way to the Upper East Side, got out, ran to the Ninety-second Street Y, ripped off all his clothes, jumped in the pool.

STAPLES  He did four?

CHASE  Four pinks, yep.

STAPLES  . . . Did he have a gun or something?

CHASE  Gunless.

STAPLES  Wow.

CHASE  I know, right?

STAPLES  Could he like *swim*?

CHASE  Good question.

*They watch.* CHASE *removes his hand from his pants.*

STAPLES  I took two once.

CHASE  Pinks?

STAPLES  Uh-huh.

CHASE  Halfs or fulls?

STAPLES  Fulls.

CHASE  Two full pinks?

STAPLES  One right after the other.

CHASE  When?

STAPLES  Coupla days ago.

CHASE  Was I around?

STAPLES  Yeah, you were around.

CHASE  Do you remember where?

STAPLES  You were in your room with that plastic thing.

CHASE  Oh. Right on.

*They watch.*

CHASE  Anything weird happen?

STAPLES  Tried to steal a Christmas tree.

CHASE  Whoa.

*Finer Noble Gases*

STAPLES  I know, right?

CHASE  Like *steal* steal?

STAPLES  Like theft, dude.

CHASE  Where?

STAPLES  New Kmart by the Six Train.

CHASE  They serve breakfast there. Eggs and stuff.

*They watch.*

CHASE  You get caught?

STAPLES  Yeah. Two undercover security guards. They were cool.

*They watch.*

CHASE  What kinda tree was it?

STAPLES  It was a blue tree, Chase. Smelled like chewing gum.

*They watch.*

CHASE  Blue like what kinda blue?

STAPLES  Blue like when the tape pops out of the VCR blue.
Kinda violety.

CHASE  Nice imagery, Staples.

STAPLES  Thanks, Chase.

*They watch.*

STAPLES  I thought it would look good next to the keyboard.
Some lights. A wreath maybe.

CHASE  They got wreaths over at the hardware store on Seventh.

STAPLES  The one with all the paint.

CHASE  Little green wreaths.

STAPLES  We coulda got one and painted it blue.

CHASE  To match the tree.

STAPLES  And the pills.

*They watch.*

CHASE  It's cool that it was scented.

STAPLES  I know, right?

*They watch.*

STAPLES  Sometimes you look at something. You weigh it in your mind. Like a rock. Or a gallon of paint. French coins are like that.

CHASE  Francs.

STAPLES  Yeah, stuff in your pocket feels better when it's heavy . . . But the really weird thing . . .

CHASE  Yeah?

STAPLES  The really weird thing is that I like *wanted* to get caught.

CHASE  You wanted it.

STAPLES  I did, Chase, I did. I thought maybe they'd yell at me. Stuff like (*as if invaded*), *Stand up straight!* Or, *Look at me when I'm talking to you!*

CHASE  Did they?

STAPLES  Nu-uh.

CHASE  What'd they do?

STAPLES  They put me in a room. There was this big mirror. A few metal chairs. This woman came in and gave me a glass of water. Then she put the tree up and left me alone with it. I think they were studying me on the other side of the mirror.

CHASE  Like *studying* studying?

STAPLES  Uh-huh.

CHASE  What do you think they were studying?

STAPLES  Probably my mind. The like waves and stuff.

CHASE  Huh.

*They watch.*

CHASE  Did the woman like *do* anything to the tree after she put it up?

STAPLES *thinks.*

STAPLES  Um. I don't think I understand your question, dude.

CHASE  I don't know. I guess I'm asking about ornaments and stuff. Popcorn. Like did she *decorate* it.

STAPLES  Nu-uh.

CHASE  Huh.

*They watch.*

STAPLES  It was pretty weird. Lonely.

CHASE  Did like *you* do anything?

STAPLES  Um. Uh-uh. I *felt* like doing something, though. Like getting up and whirling my arms. Or just jumping up and down a few times.

CHASE  Did you get busted?

STAPLES  Busted and disgusted. I called Frank the Father. He called his lawyers. They took care of it.

CHASE  Frank the Father's a lawyer, too, isn't he?

STAPLES  Lawyer. Banker. CFO. UFO.

CHASE  Unidentified Flying . . . Financial Officer.

STAPLES *imitates a UFO flying through the air. He follows it with an invisible ray gun and then mimes shooting it out of the air. They both follow its descent to the earth and watch it crash. They laugh sadly. One of them farts like a French horn.*

CHASE  Was that you or me?

STAPLES  I think it was you.

CHASE  Oh.

*They watch.*

STAPLES  I think about doing stuff but I get tired. Like more stealing. Canned fish. Little plastic things. Gum.

   Or breaking a window with my *fist!* Wrapping it with the newspaper first and then *punching!* Or kicking a garbage can!

CHASE *starts to twitch uncontrollably.*

STAPLES  (*calm now*) Dude, you're like twitching all over the place.

CHASE *twitches.*

STAPLES  That's so cool. I wish I could twitch . . . Sometimes I'll look at my hand. Like at a finger. And I'll say to it, I'll say, *Move*. And it will.

CHASE  Motor skills.

STAPLES  That's how aliens must do stuff. I mean if they're in a human body. Cause they don't have the muscle memories. So they have to tell themselves what to do. Hands and feet. Arms. They'll say, *Walk, legs*. Like in their language. They'll command themselves to do it. And they'll just start walking places. So there's more lag time with aliens. Cause they don't have the memories.

CHASE*'s twitching punctuates into an explosive bicep muscle.*

CHASE  Feel my muscle.

STAPLES  Feel your muscle?

CHASE  Yeah.

STAPLES  Like *feel* feel it?

CHASE  Sure.

STAPLES  No way, dude.

CHASE  Come on, Staples, covet my power source! Feel the way my calories burn with whitehot fire!

STAPLES  That's way too close, Chase!

CHASE  Whitehot, blistering foxfire!!!

STAPLES  All I ask for is two feet!

CHASE  The truth of my muscle would crush thee!!!

CHASE *releases his muscle.*

CHASE  (*catching his breath*) You feel so much on the pinks. So much feeling.

STAPLES  The blues are cool, too.

CHASE  The blues give you the blues. Like someone's inside you playing a harmonica.

STAPLES  Someone really really small.

*They watch.*

CHASE  Yeah. And then there's the pissers.

STAPLES  The pissers give you the runs.

CHASE  But they make you feel stuff.

STAPLES  Oh, they're total feelwhores.

CHASE  Like the pinks but quicker.

STAPLES  A little hotter, too. Like plants.

CHASE  Like plants?

STAPLES  Yeah, plants. Like in a greenhouse. How they do that thing to the Sun. Trap it or something.

CHASE  . . . Photosynthesis.

*The front door opens.* LYNCH *enters, closes the door. He is thirty, big, heavily bearded. He wears layers and layers of old sweats, batting gloves, a scarf, a dockworker's skullcap, construction boots, a weight belt. He is exhausted, hunched, slow-moving. There is the sense that he has to search for every step. While crossing, he stops behind the sofa and is lured by the TV. He watches. Only the sound of the shrieking animal.*

*After a moment,* LYNCH *takes a few long strides toward the TV and then kicks it in.*

*The* MAN ON THE FLOOR *rises and crosses upstage. He takes his underwear down and begins urinating thoroughly into a broken tom-tom drum.*

*Finer Noble Gases*

LYNCH *turns, stares at* CHASE *and* STAPLES *for a moment, and exits to the back of the apartment, closes a door.*

CHASE *and* STAPLES *stare at the kicked-in TV, while the* MAN ON THE FLOOR *continues to urinate.*

STAPLES  Chase?
CHASE  Yeah, Staples?
STAPLES  I don't know what to like um *do*.
CHASE  Either do I.

STAPLES *turns to* CHASE.

STAPLES  I'm getting up!
CHASE  Yeah?
STAPLES  Yeah, I'm getting up!

*He doesn't move.*

CHASE  Maybe count to three or something.
STAPLES  Good idea.
CHASE  I'll count for you.
STAPLES  Okay.
CHASE  Ready?
STAPLES  Yeah, I'm ready. Go 'head.
CHASE  One. Two. Three.

STAPLES *rocks himself forward and off the sofa. He lurches slightly, rights himself.*

ADAM RAPP

*The* MAN ON THE FLOOR *finishes urinating, pulls his underwear up, crosses to a spot near the chair, lies down.*

CHASE  You okay?
STAPLES  Yeah, yeah, I'm good.

STAPLES *turns and crosses to the front door like some kind of lost and forlorn spaceman. He stares at the surveillance monitor and then lifts his arm and turns it on. It issues a vague, bluish-white screen, a few obscure lines.* STAPLES *attempts to wave the light from the monitor toward the TV, as if it will somehow cause it to work again.* CHASE *joins him and they wave with great fervor. They stop and watch the TV for a moment.*

CHASE  It's not working.
STAPLES  Not really, right?
CHASE  Nu-uh.

STAPLES *crosses back to the sofa, sits.*

STAPLES  We could like watch Mike the Monitor.
CHASE  We could.
STAPLES  Maybe we should move the davenport. Make it easier to see.
CHASE  Good idea.

*They stare at each other a moment.*

STAPLES  One. Two. Three.

STAPLES *rolls over his arm of the sofa and begins budging it toward the* *monitor.* CHASE *never actually gets off the sofa and attempts to move it* *by using whatever force he can generate by charging and ramming into* *one of its arms. They surf-scoot-pivot the sofa so that it faces the* *surveillance monitor.* CHASE *sits back down, exhausted. They watch* *the monitor.*

CHASE  It's not bad.
STAPLES  Not too bad.
CHASE  I like how it's kinda blank.
STAPLES  Yeah. The blankness.
CHASE  It's like snow.
STAPLES  It is kinda.
CHASE  Like a little box of snow.
STAPLES  A little box fulla snowballs.

*They watch.*

CHASE  But it's not the same!
STAPLES  I know, right?!
CHASE  I keep expecting things!
STAPLES  Yeah, Chase, me, too!
CHASE  Like a little caribou to appear!
STAPLES  I know, I know!
CHASE  And the rhino!!
STAPLES  How those birds were just sitting on his back like someone put em there!!

*They stare at each other.*

CHASE  One. Two. Three.

STAPLES *rises off the sofa, and returns it to its original position. Again,* CHASE *never actually touches the floor and uses the same charging-ramming method. After the sofa is re-positioned, they sit, exhausted.*

CHASE *suddenly charges to* STAPLES*'s end of the sofa, violently pukes over the side, smothering* STAPLES *with his body. After a moment, he thaws from the hurling, wipes his mouth, returns to his side.*

CHASE  Should I call Doug the Dad?
STAPLES  Call Doug the Dad. If it doesn't work I'll call Frank the Father.

CHASE *starts to burrow in the cracks of the sofa, searching for his cell phone. After a moment, he realizes that it is on the chair.* STAPLES *reaches into his pocket, lends him his cell phone.* CHASE *attempts to dial the number, but can't remember it. He hands the cell phone back to* STAPLES *and then lunges for the coffee table rather Olympically, and then, without ever touching the ground, manages to traverse the space between the sofa and the chair, using whatever means necessary: the coffee table, the ottoman, etc. It should be an enormous feat. He winds up securing his cell phone rather miraculously, sits on the ottoman, speed dials, waits.*

CHASE  Hey, Daddy? It's Chase . . . Hey Daddy. How's it going? How's business? . . . Good, good . . .
    What do I want? Well, nothing, Daddy. Just calling to say Hey. Hey and how's it going and how's Mary the Mom and all that . . . Oh, things are great. Really great.
    Yeah, it's getting cold out, I think. Pretty cold. Scarves and mittens, you know? . . .

*Finer Noble Gases*

Oh the band is *so* good. It's been a real productive period. We're writing songs like crazy . . . Oh, everything. Vocals. Rhythm guitar. Some very clever leads now and then. Keyboards. A little drums here and there, rat-a-tat-tat, percussion, you know? I'll send you a tape . . . Sure, sure . . . Yeah, I got the check. I totally got it. Yeah, thanks, Daddy . . .

Well, there was one thing, Daddy. One small thing . . . Yeah . . . Yeah, I know . . . Well, it's pretty small, small as a kittycat, but it's important. Really really kinda huge and important . . . Well, our TV got messed up somehow . . . Yeah, the old Trinitron . . . Well, I don't know. It's like there's a big hole in it . . . In the screen . . . Well not a *hole* hole, more like a black um *void*. Yeah, a black void in the middle . . .

Could I maybe like use the credit card? . . . I know, I know . . . Well, we *do* need it, Daddy. Cause we're thinking about shooting a video . . . Yeah . . . And we need something to watch it on. I could just buzz over to the Wiz, you know? They got great deals over there. They might even deliver. (*he nods to* STAPLES, *smiles*)

No? . . . Oh . . . You sure, dude? Okay. Okay, Daddy . . .

Yeah, I'm working. Working on the music, you know? Art's a full-time job. No compensation yet, but there will be. Big things ahead. Nothing but the sky . . .

Yeah, sure I'll come home for a few days . . . Maybe next month . . . I'll just jump on the Metro-North. A little northbound train action.

Okay, Daddy . . . Me, too . . . Tell Mom I say Hey . . . I know, I know . . . Sure . . . I'll send that tape off.

*He turns the phone off, slips it back into his pocket.*

CHASE  Your turn, dude. Frank the Father.

STAPLES *dials his cell phone, waits. After a moment he starts to make pig sounds into the phone. Pigs, monkeys, and sheep. He stops, turns the phone off, puts it back in his pocket, looks at* CHASE.

CHASE  Voicemail?

STAPLES *nods.*

*The sound of a door closing. Moments later,* LYNCH *appears from the back of the apartment. He is dressed in an enormous snowmobile suit. He steps slowly into the room as though he isn't sure where he is heading, stands very still.*

CHASE  Alaska man.
STAPLES  Glacier guy.
CHASE  What's with the snowsuit?
LYNCH  It's gettin cold.
CHASE  Yeah?
LYNCH  Sposed to get in the teens tonight.
STAPLES  Whoa.
CHASE  Better turn the heat up.
LYNCH  Things aren't workin out so well. It's better if there's snow when that happens.

CHASE *and* LYNCH *stare at each other. An awkward pause.*

CHASE  Where you goin, dude?
LYNCH  Get somethin for my toe.
CHASE  What's wrong with your toe?
LYNCH  It's numb.
CHASE  Like *numb* numb?

*Finer Noble Gases*                                                      199

LYNCH  Uh-huh.

STAPLES  It's prolly from the TV.

LYNCH  Meaning?

STAPLES  Oh, nothing. It's just that you like totally kicked it in and such.

LYNCH  Felt like the right thing to do. The perfect time, you know? (*as if invaded*) IT'S MONSTER MADNESS AT THE KIEL AUDITORIUM BIG TRUCKS *BIG BIG* TRUCKS TRUCKS SO BIG OTHER TRUCKS CAN RIDE AROUND INSIDE OF THEM!!!

*The explosion sends* LYNCH *across the room, somewhere near the keyboard. He is oddly joined to a microphone, stares at it confused for a second, re-sets it on the stand.*

*CHASE and* STAPLES *stare at each other.* LYNCH *crosses to the neon beer sign, turns it on, then touches the keyboard for a moment.*

LYNCH  (*a reaching out*) I feel really far away from things. Like everything's gettin smaller.

*Nobody moves.*

CHASE  Um. How was like work, dude?

LYNCH  Okay.

CHASE  What kinda stuff you move?

LYNCH  Sofas. Bookcases. Beds. Some statues.

CHASE  Like *statue* statues?

LYNCH  Men, women. Men mostly.

STAPLES  Were they like nude?

LYNCH  Yeah.

STAPLES  Any hot bods?

LYNCH *reaches into one of his pockets and removes a marble breast.*

STAPLES  *Dude.*

CHASE  *Dude!* Gettin a little on the *side!*

LYNCH *starts to slowly move the breast through the air, almost dancing with it. He hums a melodious tune.* CHASE *and* STAPLES *collaborate a bit.* LYNCH *blows into the breast as if it is a conch shell, making his way toward* CHASE. *He places the breast on* CHASE*'s head, his face, his beard. What seems like fun starts to get a little scary as he uses the marble breast to force* CHASE*'s head into the cushion of the chair.*

LYNCH  (*releasing* CHASE*'s head*) Can't have it!

CHASE  Cool.

LYNCH  (*to* STAPLES) You either!

STAPLES  Hey, that's totally cool.

LYNCH *puts the marble breast back in his pocket, crosses to the TV, sits on it.*

LYNCH  I used to know a lot more stuff. (*to* CHASE) When we were in school, you know?

CHASE  Sure.

LYNCH  Facts mostly. I was good with facts.

CHASE  Facts are good.

STAPLES  Yeah, dude. Facts are totally good.

LYNCH *crosses to the window.*

*Finer Noble Gases*

LYNCH  I've been keeping a brick in my pocket. Left pocket.

CHASE  A brick and a tit.

LYNCH  Found it in the basement.

CHASE  The basement?

STAPLES  Like the *basement* basement?

LYNCH  Uh-huh.

CHASE  What were you like doing down in the basement?

LYNCH  Lookin for things. Gettin stuff together.

CHASE  Things?

STAPLES  Stuff?

LYNCH  Things and stuff. Lookin and gettin. Pretty much in that order. (*to* CHASE) There's all these robots everywhere.

STAPLES *tries to make himself invisible.*

CHASE  Robots?

LYNCH  Uh-huh. Millions of em. A hundred million.

CHASE  Cool.

LYNCH  (*to* STAPLES) They're just layin there like they're sleepin. A hundred million robots.

CHASE *and* STAPLES *stare at each other.* LYNCH *turns, crosses to the* MAN ON THE FLOOR. *From his mouth he drops a slow gob of spit on him. The* MAN ON THE FLOOR *doesn't stir.* LYNCH *watches him for a moment and then crosses to the front door. Before he exits, he removes a brick from his left pocket and smashes through the front of the surveillance monitor.*

LYNCH  (*another reaching out*) Bye.

CHASE  Bye.

STAPLES  Bye, dude.

LYNCH  Washington was a good president. But Lincoln was better. You can tell cause of the pictures. His beard and stuff.

LYNCH *exits. His footfalls can be heard descending the stairs.* CHASE *and* STAPLES *sit very still.*

CHASE  I have an idea.

STAPLES  Yeah?

CHASE  Heldinwell.

STAPLES  *Heldinwell?*

CHASE  The guy who lives downstairs. The weird guy in number three.

STAPLES  What about him?

CHASE  *He's* got a TV.

STAPLES  You're saying?

CHASE  We should totally take it.

STAPLES  Like rob him?

CHASE  Sure. I'll invite him up and while he's under my narrative spell you can use the fire escape and bust into his apartment and snag his TV.

STAPLES  Good idea.

CHASE  I know, right?

STAPLES  Sneaky.

CHASE  It's totally sneaky.

CHASE *starts to make his way back to the sofa via the ottoman and coffee table route, as before.*

STAPLES  . . . So, um, can I like ask a question?

CHASE  (*transitioning from ottoman to coffee table*) Sure.

STAPLES  Why do you get to be the narrative spell guy?

CHASE  Cause, dude, I'm a good conversationalist.

STAPLES  You are?

CHASE  Dude, I'm such a good conversationalist. My words and images. My use of metaphor and freakish nouns.

STAPLES  Are you trying to say that I'm like *not good* at images and freakish nouns?

CHASE  No.

STAPLES  Cause I can totally paint pictures with words, Chase. You know I'm so good at that.

CHASE  You are, you are.

STAPLES  I'm like a metaphor *factory.*

CHASE  (*secure on the coffee table now*) That's true, Staples. That's totally true. But where you're the factory I'm like the quality control division. I make the metaphor a little more slippery. I add the salt and pepper. The spicy spices. I'm like the quality control *chef* who takes on the metaphor as soon as it comes off the assembly line.

STAPLES  But, dude, I—

CHASE  *Plus*, you're on the blues. I'm on the pinks!

STAPLES  I'm such a good conversationalist, Chase. I have a large assortment of words and ideas.

CHASE  Why do you think I like hanging with you so much? Besides, you're the one who's always getting locked out and coming in through the window.

STAPLES  What's that supposed to mean?

CHASE  Nothing. Just that you're more familiar with the ways and means of the fire escape. It's one of the things you're really really good at.

STAPLES  . . . Maybe.

CHASE  I'll call him.

CHASE *leaps from the coffee table, lands on his side of the sofa rather impressively, pulls his cell phone out of his pocket, dials, waits.*

CHASE  Yes. I'd like the number of a *Heldinwell* on East Tenth Street in Manhattan . . . Cool. (*he winks at* STAPLES) Hello. Is this Mister Heldinwell? . . . It is? . . . Oh, hey. This is Chase. Chase Fitzsimmons, your upstairs neighbor in apartment five . . .

Hey! How's it going? . . . Good, good.

Well, anyway, the reason I'm calling is cause I sorta hurt my back real bad today . . . Yeah, I slipped on the ice and landed on the old sacro*sternum* . . . Yeah, slipped and fell like an old person. *Whooop!* . . . Oh, the sacro*sternum*, that thing under the spinal canal . . . Yeah, in the lumber division . . . Anyway, I'm on these killer pain pills. These big pharmaceutical hockey pucks. And the thing is, I'm feeling a little fuzzed-out and insecure and both my roommates are away for the weekend. You see, I keep thinking someone's *behind me*. It's pretty bad . . .

STAPLES *slowly turns around and checks behind the sofa.*

CHASE  Well, I know it sounds silly, but I was wondering if you wouldn't mind coming upstairs and entertaining me for a while. I keep wanting to turn around real fast but I know I'm not supposed to cause of my discs and stuff. The lumber division of the spinal canal is quite neurologically and anatomically sensitive . . . You would? Cool, cool. I'd really appreciate that . . . Yeah, I just thought we could talk for a while. Shoot the breeze, you know? Get to know each other neighbor to neighbor. Upstairs to downstairs. Man to man . . .

God, I *so* appreciate that . . . It's these pills, you know? I think I took too many. I almost broke down and called a film festival—

STAPLES  Dude!

CHASE  I mean *hospital*! . . . Oh, come up as soon as you can.
ASAP. The door's open. Yeah, I keep wanting to turn around.
Thanks, guy. I so appreciate it. See you in a few.

*He hangs up.*

STAPLES  Nice?

CHASE  Oh, totally nice. Kinda shy.

STAPLES  Huh.

*A pause.*

CHASE  Um. He's probably like on his way up the stairs right
now.

STAPLES  You think it's gonna snow?

CHASE  I don't know, Staples.

STAPLES  I used to make snowmen. Big ones. With hats and
stuff. Scarves. I'd sit next to them and we'd memorize baseball
cards. Height. Weight. Hometown. We'd do state capitals, too.
Albany. Tallahassee. Jefferson City . . . Do you know the state
capital of Illinois?!

CHASE  Sure, Staples.

STAPLES  What is it?!

CHASE  It's Springfield, isn't it?

STAPLES *stares off.*

CHASE  You okay, buddy?

STAPLES  I keep thinking about the caribou. How it reminds
me of all this stuff I can't remember. Like being on a school

bus. The way the seats smelled. Stuff like that. And Magilla Gorilla!

CHASE  What about him?

STAPLES  I can't remember if he was a walrus or an Alaskan snow pony!!!

CHASE  Um. I think he was a gorilla, Staples.

STAPLES  Yeah?

CHASE  I'm pretty sure about that one.

STAPLES  I was thinking about getting a job today. Doing something with my hands. Catching fish. Making things. Little wooden toys.

CHASE  Toys are cool.

STAPLES  (*a little terrified*) I had this dream last night that I was a robot. Big metal robot—

CHASE  Yeah, you were crying—

STAPLES  I was crying but nothing was coming out. I could feel the crying in my throat but no tears—

CHASE  And you didn't have any balls—

STAPLES  I didn't have any balls. Instead I had a light switch! I kept trying to turn it on—

CHASE  But all it did was make this buzzing noise.

STAPLES  I was going to this graveyard. Where all the other robots were buried. And I found this flower. It was pink. A tulip, I think. I ate it. It made me feel better.

CHASE  Look, if all goes well, I bet we'll get to see what happens to the caribou.

STAPLES  You think so?

CHASE  I *totally* think so.

STAPLES  I'd like that.

CHASE  Me, too, Staples. Me, too. You want me to count to three?

*Finer Noble Gases*

STAPLES  Would you?
CHASE  Sure, buddy.

*He squares his body to* STAPLES.

CHASE  One. Two. Three.

STAPLES *rocks forward and off the sofa, lurches a bit, rights himself,*
*and then stares at the bowls of pills. He goes for a pink.*

STAPLES  Maybe I should take a pink.
CHASE  (*standing on the sofa*) I don't know, Staples! Maybe
another blue. Keep the colors together.
STAPLES  Right.

STAPLES *reaches down, grabs a blue pill, puts it in his mouth,*
*swallows. Then he turns and crosses to the back of the apartment.*

CHASE *stretches out on the sofa, his head opposite the front door. He*
*puts a pillow under his knees, affects the posture of a back injury*
*victim. Moments later,* STAPLES *appears wearing a snowmobile suit,*
*similar to* LYNCH's, *but a different color. He crosses to the stage left*
*window, attempts to lift it. It doesn't budge. He tries again. No luck.*

STAPLES  It's frozen shut.

*A knock at the door.*

CHASE *and* STAPLES *stare at each other, stare at the door, back at each*
*other.*

ADAM RAPP

STAPLES *tries to lift the window again, screaming now. It still won't budge.*

CHASE *shouts at him to hide in the back of the apartment. He uses strange, guttural noises and a kind of primitive gibberish.*

STAPLES *moves as quickly as he can down the hall to the back of the apartment, like an astronaut in need of a toilet.*

*Another knock.*

CHASE  Come in.

*The door opens very slowly. A nondescript man enters. He is thirtyish, clean-shaven. He wears a plain gray suit and a vague tie. He wears black, thick-rimmed glasses. He carries a half-dozen tulips arranged in a glass vase. He leaves the door open. He is painfully shy, but can get into the occasional groove just like anybody else.*

GRAY  Are you Chase?
CHASE  I am. You must be . . .
GRAY  Um. Gray. Gray Heldinwell. From apartment three.
CHASE  Well, hey there, neighbor.
GRAY  Hey.
CHASE  How's it going?
GRAY  Pretty good.
CHASE  Well, come in, come in.
GRAY  Thanks.

GRAY *closes the door and steps carefully into the room.*

GRAY  I brought you these.

*He crosses to* CHASE, *hands him the tulips.*

CHASE  (*amazed at their vividness*) Flowers!
GRAY  Tulips.
CHASE  Wow. Um. Thanks . . . *Gray?*
GRAY  Yeah, Gray.
CHASE  . . . Hey, Gray!
GRAY  Hey!

GRAY *stands there awkwardly.* CHASE *stares at the tulips, is strangely transfixed. Perhaps he licks one. Gray takes them away.*

GRAY  (*setting them on the coffee table*) When I was in the hospital Nurse H would always bring me tulips.
CHASE  Nice.
GRAY  Nurse H and I had similar tastes in things. We both like travel literature. And slanted rain. And knives.
CHASE  Knives?
GRAY  Yeah, we both have knife collections.
CHASE  What kinda knives?
GRAY  Nurse H has two dozen Willie Stonetooth Redpoints. I have a set of Captain Diablo Throwing Blades.
CHASE  Wow.
GRAY  You can only get Captain Diablos south of the border. They come in sets of ten. Varying weights and flight speeds.
CHASE  Cool.

GRAY *continues to stand.*

CHASE  Be seated earthling.

GRAY *stares at the empty stage left chair for a moment, then at the* MAN ON THE FLOOR.

GRAY  I thought you said your roommates were out of town.
CHASE  They are.
GRAY  (*pointing to the* MAN ON THE FLOOR) Who's that?
CHASE  Oh, that's Speed.
GRAY  Speed?
CHASE  Yeah, Speed. He just got here. Surprise visit.
GRAY  Oh. What's he doing?
CHASE  He's just sorta hanging out.

GRAY *turns toward the door.*

CHASE  Take a seat!

GRAY *stops, considers the chair again, turns toward the drum set, indicates that perhaps that would be a better choice, sits on a crate, accidentally steps on the kick drum pedal, jumps like a jackrabbit, practically annihilates the drum set, an explosion of sound. After a moment, he regains his composure, sits on the crate again.*

GRAY  So how'd you hurt your back?
CHASE  Well, I slipped and . . . Well, you know— (*a vague gesture*) Whooop!
GRAY  (*feebly imitating the gesture*) Whooop.

*Pause.*

*Finer Noble Gases*

GRAY  That's what I was in the hospital for.

CHASE  What?

GRAY  My back.

CHASE  Really.

GRAY  They almost had to do invasive surgery. Pinched nerve.

CHASE  Ouch.

GRAY  Sciatic node between L-five and S-one. The pain was pretty excruciating. Two days of traction and a few months of physical therapy. I'm okay now.

CHASE  Wow.

GRAY  Yeah, I had to lay on the floor a lot . . . Did they medicate in triplicate?

CHASE  Um . . .

GRAY  Anti-inflammatory, muscle relaxer, painkiller?

CHASE  Oh. Well, um, yeah, actually. All of the above.

GRAY  The Carisoprodol is pretty good. They give you that?

CHASE  They did. Yes. They *did* give me that.

GRAY  It's great right before bed. Especially coupled with the Hydrocodone. They probably gave you that, too, right?

CHASE  How'd you know?

GRAY  It's good for nerve pain. Hydrocodone's a synthetic narcotic. Generic spin-off of codeine. Well, they *say* codeine but it's actually closer to morphine.

CHASE  Wow, Gray, you're like pharmacologically blessed.

GRAY  The Naproxen's nothing to write home about, but an anti-inflammatory's an anti-inflammatory. Seen one you've seen them all.

CHASE  You're so right.

GRAY  (*rising off the crate, crossing toward the sofa*) I still have a pretty good relationship with my orthopedic guy. Doctor P, NYU Medical Center.

CHASE  Yeah, Doctor P, NYU Medical. Over there at . . .

GRAY  Thirty-first and First.

CHASE  Thirty-first and First. Right, right.

GRAY  You should be okay in forty-eight to seventy-two hours. As long as it's not a hot disc. You don't have a hot disc do you?

CHASE  Oh, no way. My discs are totally cool and non-hot.

GRAY  Then you're probably in pretty good shape.

CHASE  God I hope so.

*While* GRAY *sits, someone farts like a French horn. Awkward pause.*

CHASE  So, how long have you been in the building, Gray?

GRAY  A while. I just signed another lease.

CHASE  You like the neighborhood?

GRAY  Of course.

CHASE  We got the park. The Russian Bath House. That funny hat shop across the street.

GRAY  That hat shop's not funny.

CHASE  Oh. I was just saying—

GRAY  I don't think it's funny at all.

CHASE  Okay.

*Pause.*

*Someone farts again.*

CHASE  Was that you or me?

GRAY  I think it was you.

CHASE  Oh.

GRAY  (*collaboratively*) Maybe it was Speed?

CHASE  Right on.

*They share forced laughter.*

CHASE  Care for a pill? We have blues, pinks, and yellows. We call the yellows pissers.

GRAY *rises, considers the pills for a moment, backs away.*

GRAY  No thanks.

*Suddenly,* STAPLES *appears from the back of the apartment. He is still wearing the snowmobile suit. He is also wearing a hood now and snow goggles. He walks up to the window very quickly, somehow trying to make himself invisible. He tries to lift it again. He is successful this time. He crawls through the window, closes it behind him, and disappears down the fire escape.* GRAY *is quite startled.*

GRAY  Who was that?

CHASE  Huh?

GRAY  That man.

CHASE  What man?

GRAY  The one in the snowsuit.

CHASE  I didn't see anyone.

GRAY  Oh. Well, a man in a snowsuit just walked through your living room, opened the window, and exited down the fire escape.

CHASE  Really?

GRAY  Yeah.

CHASE  Are you sure, dude?

GRAY  Sure I'm sure.

GRAY *rises, crosses toward the window, creeps up on it very slowly, seizes one of the dinette chairs, then looks out quickly. After a moment, he re-sets the chair, crosses to* CHASE.

GRAY  He's not there anymore.

GRAY *crosses toward the door.*

CHASE  *Sit, sit, sit!*

GRAY *crosses to the living room chair, confused, regards* SPEED *for a moment, sits.* CHASE *shifts to the other side of the sofa. He feigns pain.* GRAY *rises and attempts to help him, awkwardly reaching toward him, but never actually touching him.* CHASE *settles with his head against the stage right side of the sofa, still feigning pain.* GRAY *accidentally falls into* CHASE's *lap face-first.* GRAY *stands very quickly. An awkward moment.* GRAY *attempts to regain his composure, makes his way back to the chair, sits.*

CHASE  What do you do, Gray?

GRAY  . . . Excuse me?

CHASE  What.

GRAY  I'm not gay.

CHASE  Huh?

GRAY  You think I'm gay?

CHASE  Dude, what are you talking ab—

GRAY  (*standing*) Didn't you just ask me if I was gay?

*Finer Noble Gases*                                           215

CHASE  Um, no. I asked you—

GRAY  Are you trying to take advantage of me?!

CHASE  All I said was—

GRAY  Cause I won't let that happen! I know karate!

GRAY *explodes with an exhibition of karate, approaching* CHASE *rather aggressively,* CHASE *stands on the sofa suddenly, somehow defusing the onslaught.*

CHASE  I *said* WHAT-DO-YOU-DO, GRAY!

GRAY  Oh.

CHASE  WHOA!

GRAY  . . . Sorry.

CHASE  NO ONE IS TAKING ADVANTAGE OF ANYONE!

GRAY  Oh. I'm so sorry.

CHASE, *suddenly realizing that he is standing with little effort, begins feigning pain again, crumples down to the sofa.* GRAY *attempts to help him again, but* CHASE *wards him off.*

GRAY *turns to the chair, where* SPEED *has managed to drape his arm over the cushion.*

GRAY  (*crossing back to the chair*) I work for a prominent financial institution.

CHASE  Like a bank?

GRAY  It's a little more complicated than that.

CHASE  Okay.

GRAY  (*removing* SPEED's *arm*) I'm involved with the information side of things. Sorting and processing. I deal with data.

CHASE  You crunch numbers.

GRAY I do. I do crunch numbers. But I do so much more than just crunch them.

CHASE Like what?

GRAY Well, I soften them too. I soften *and* crunch. And there's a fair amount of spreading as well.

CHASE Spreading?

GRAY Sure.

CHASE Like spreadsheets?

GRAY Just spreading.

CHASE Huh.

*Suddenly,* GRAY *whirls around in the chair really fast, desperately looks over both shoulders, stops, turns to* CHASE.

GRAY You sure you didn't see that guy in the snowsuit?

CHASE Pretty sure, Gray.

SPEED *suddenly pulls a deflated blowup doll from underneath the cushion of the chair, screams, bounds apelike toward the hallway, punches a hole in the Sheetrock.* GRAY *seizes the ottoman, raises it over his head as if to strike, but doesn't.* SPEED *stares at him for a moment.*

SPEED Magilla Gorilla.

SPEED *crosses to the back of the apartment singing the first few verses of the "Magilla Gorilla" theme song, disappears.* GRAY *regains his composure, sets the ottoman down, a little invigorated, sits.*

GRAY (*referring to* SPEED) You're in a band.

CHASE I am.

GRAY I'll bet you didn't think I knew that.

CHASE  Well—

GRAY  When you've lived in the building as long as I have you pick up on certain things. The walls are filled with information, trust me on that one. You just have to know how to listen.

CHASE  Huh.

GRAY  What are you guys called again?

CHASE  Well, we were called Lester's Surprise, but then we changed it to Lester's Sister. And then it was just Lester. I can't remember what we were after that.

GRAY  Less.

CHASE  Excuse me?

GRAY  I think you were called Less after that.

CHASE  Really.

GRAY  Uh-huh.

CHASE  Like *less* less?

GRAY  L-E-S-S. You guys used to put posters up all over the place. "Less is More."

CHASE  Huh.


GRAY *rises, crosses to the vase of tulips, pulls it close.*


GRAY  Yeah, I used to get out some. People to see, places to go, you know?

CHASE  Sure.

GRAY  But not so much lately. Too much to do. Projects. Big plans. Lots of ideas.


GRAY *sets the vase of tulips on top of the TV.*


CHASE  Huh.

GRAY  I have this lamp. White cut glass. It has a swan's neck. The head is shaped like tulips. Ten of them. A bouquet. Gives a real nice soft glow. An astral glow. I think they put argon gas in the bulbs. At least it says that on the little tag. I found it in that old thrift shop across the street. It hardly cost anything.

CHASE  . . . Uh-huh?

GRAY  I'll just stare at it for hours. I'm not sure why. Sometimes I think I'm waiting for it to talk to me. Like the tulips will tell me what to do.

CHASE  Huh.


*Pause.*


GRAY  I was approached on the street today.

CHASE  Approached?

GRAY  Yeah, approached. Carefully approached.

CHASE  By who?

GRAY  Two men. Very important men.

CHASE  When you say "approached"—

GRAY  They just emerged. The way birds emerge.

CHASE  Birds.

GRAY  Large, dark birds. You mind if I turn the light off?

CHASE  Not at all.


GRAY *vigilantly crosses to the neon beer sign, sets a chair to reach it, stands on the chair, turns the sign off.*


CHASE  So what did these "very important" men *do* after they um "emerged"?

GRAY  (*still standing on the chair*) Handed me some pamphlets. Took my information.

CHASE  What kinda information?

GRAY  Personal things. Height. Weight. Social Security number. Stuff like that.

CHASE  Wow.

GRAY  They took a Polaroid, too.

CHASE  Friendly.

GRAY  Yeah, I was wearing my hat.

CHASE  Your hat?

GRAY  From Millie's Millinery.

CHASE  What's that?

GRAY  Um. That hat shop across the street.

CHASE  Right.

GRAY  (*stepping down from chair*) There's a meeting tomorrow. Big meeting.

CHASE  With those guys who "approached" you.

GRAY  I'm not supposed to talk about it!

CHASE  Okay.

GRAY  They gave me some money.

CHASE  To not talk about it.

GRAY  A lot of money. In a shoebox. It was heavier than if shoes were in it.

CHASE  Cool.

GRAY  I think a certain government official is in danger, let's just say that. And like they said, he deserves to be.

CHASE  Sure.

GRAY  I'm willing to go to certain lengths.

CHASE  Of course.

GRAY  Long Daniel's going to be speaking on Public Access in a few minutes.

CHASE  Who's that?

GRAY  Leader of the movement.

CHASE  One of the "money dudes"?

GRAY Long Daniel's the visionary. They work for him. He's the guy in all the literature. (*referring to the TV*) Public Access. Channel Sixteen.

CHASE I'd turn it on, Gray, but our TV's like totally cashed.

*Suddenly,* STAPLES *appears in the window with a large TV.* CHASE *sees him.*

GRAY Then I'll go get mine.

CHASE Your TV?

GRAY Sure.

CHASE Oh, no, you don't have to do that!

GRAY But I want to.

CHASE But it's so inconvenient. And I wouldn't want you to hurt your back agai—

GRAY You don't like me.

CHASE Oh, that's so not true!

GRAY You find me repellent.

GRAY *crumples down to the ottoman, almost prostrate on the floor now.*

CHASE Gray. Hey. Hey now. I find you so totally *not* repellent.

CHASE *desperately signals to* STAPLES *to take* GRAY's *TV back downstairs.* STAPLES *watches vaguely through the window for a moment, then nods, and disappears.* GRAY *checks behind him for a moment.*

GRAY (*rising, regaining his composure*) They don't talk to me at work.

CHASE They *talk* to you.

GRAY  No they don't.

CHASE  Sure they do.

GRAY  You don't know.

CHASE  People just don't *not talk* to people.

GRAY  Just because I got caught with the rubber bands.

CHASE  Rubber bands?

GRAY  A big blob of rubber bands. I couldn't help it.

CHASE  Caught doing what exactly?

GRAY *sits on the sofa.*

GRAY  I was putting them down my pants.

CHASE  Whoa.

GRAY  Sometimes I'll grab a handful. When my boss isn't looking.

CHASE  Oh. What does that like um *do?*

GRAY  It takes the loneliness away.

CHASE  Huh.

GRAY  I think about the woods sometimes. Just getting away from it all. The smell of deer. Big timber. Blackbirds in the branches.

*Pause.*

CHASE  Go get your TV, Gray.

GRAY  Okay.

GRAY *rises, slowly crosses to the front door, turns back.*

GRAY  Maybe I could just leave it up here, you know? Then I could come up and visit whenever.

CHASE  Hey, it's definitely worth discussing.

GRAY  Okay.


GRAY *turns to exit.*


CHASE  What kinda TV is it?

GRAY  Magnavox nineteen-inch stereo surroundsound with master remote.

CHASE  The kinda remote that's like heavy in your hand?

GRAY  Uh-huh.

CHASE  Totally go get it.

GRAY  Okay.

CHASE  But Gray?

GRAY  Yeah?


CHASE *moves himself to an upright position, feigning great pain. As before,* GRAY *reaches awkwardly, feebly, to help him, falls to his knees. Then suddenly, his hands find* CHASE's *hair, his face, his beard. It's more about the relief of physical human connection than anything sexual. Nonetheless, another awkward moment.*


CHASE  Promise me you'll be careful.

GRAY  I will, Chase.


GRAY *rises, crosses to the door, stops, and turns back one more time.*


GRAY  Um. I've never told anyone about that before.

CHASE  About what?

GRAY  The rubber band thing.


GRAY *turns and exits.*


*Finer Noble Gases*                                                            223

*A moment later,* LYNCH *enters. There is ice in his beard. He is carrying a small* MALE CHILD, *perhaps six or seven and bundled in a hooded winter parka, scarf, and rollerblades. On the backs of both Rollerblades, the name "Pete" is spelled out in colorful decals. He is not wearing pants. One of his legs is discolored. His arms hang lifelessly at his sides.* LYNCH *is still wearing his snowmobile suit. He is also holding a black garbage bag containing a few lightweight objects.*

LYNCH  Hey.

CHASE  Hey, dude . . . Who's that?

LYNCH  Pete.

CHASE  Oh. Where's he from?

LYNCH  The park.

CHASE  Like the *park* park?

LYNCH  Uh-huh.

CHASE  What were you doing in the park?

LYNCH  Just walking around.

CHASE  Walking around, huh?

LYNCH  Pretty much, yeah. The monkey bars were interesting.

CHASE  Is that where you found, um, *Pete*?

LYNCH  He was sleeping up against one of the handball courts. This dog was tryin to mess with him but I took care of that.

CHASE  Where are his, like, pants?

LYNCH  I don't know.


LYNCH *starts for the kitchen area.*


CHASE  Um, Lynch.

LYNCH  (*stopping*) Yeah?

CHASE  Pete doesn't look too good.


ADAM RAPP

LYNCH *crosses to the kitchen table, sets the* BOY *in a chair, starts the oven, opens the oven door.*

CHASE  What are you going, dude?
LYNCH  Warming him up.
CHASE  Maybe you should like take him to the hospital.
LYNCH  He's just cold. He'll be okay.

*From the plastic garbage bag* LYNCH *removes two enormous, white, foam core animal masks: one is obviously a bear mask; the other is a half-made elephant mask.*

CHASE  What are those?
LYNCH  Oh, I think Pete was making em. This one's a bear. I think the other one's sposed to be an elephant. (*putting the bear mask on*) Wanna play? You can be the elephant?
CHASE  . . . Um, how's your toe, dude?
LYNCH  It's still numb. So is my leg. And I can't feel my knee.

LYNCH *unsnaps his snowmobile suit and long underwear, pushes them down to his ankles, standing naked now. He prods his knee a bit.*

LYNCH  It's still there, right?
CHASE  Yeah, dude, it's still there.

GRAY *enters with the TV, stops suddenly.*

GRAY  Hi.
LYNCH  Hi.
GRAY  I'm Gray.

*Finer Noble Gases*

*Awkward pause.*

CHASE  Gray, this is Lynch.
GRAY  Nice to meet you, Lynch.

LYNCH *doesn't respond, just stands there, still wearing the mask.*

CHASE  (*pointing to the* BOY *seated at the kitchen table*) And that's, um, Pete.

GRAY *is confused.*

LYNCH  Pete's pretty shy.

GRAY *places the TV on the floor in front of the other one. He turns to* LYNCH.

GRAY  You're wearing a bear mask.
LYNCH  Yeah.
GRAY  And you're naked.
LYNCH  Oh. Sorry.

LYNCH *pulls his long underwear back up, stands there for a moment.*

GRAY *plugs in the TV, attaches the cable box, removes a large remote from his breast pocket, crosses to* CHASE, *almost hands it to him, then starts for the door.*

CHASE  Where you going, Gray?

ADAM RAPP

GRAY *looks at* LYNCH, *then back to* CHASE.

GRAY  Um. They called me when I was downstairs.
CHASE  They.
GRAY  *Them.*
CHASE  The "money dudes"?

GRAY *looks at* LYNCH, *and then* CHASE.

GRAY  (*careful*) The call was in reference to that
certain *government official* I was telling you about. They
need me.
CHASE  They like *need you* need you?
GRAY  They sounded professionally desperate.
CHASE  For the "money job"?
GRAY  (*finally handing* CHASE *the remote*) It's a Mission, yes. I have
to go pack my knives. I shouldn't say anything else.
CHASE  Right.
GRAY  And I can't forget my hat. Gotta go.

GRAY *is frozen.*

CHASE  Gray.
GRAY  Yes?
CHASE  Maybe you should take a pill.

GRAY *crosses to the bowl of pills.*

GRAY  You think?
CHASE  Oh, absolutely.

GRAY  Which one?

CHASE  Take a pink.

GRAY *takes a pink pill from the bowl, pops it in his mouth, then removes a nondescript mint green plastic bottle from his breast pocket, unscrews it, drinks, washing down the pill.*

CHASE  Take two, dude.

GRAY *takes another pink, washes it down.*

CHASE  Take a yellow, too.

GRAY *takes a yellow, washes it down, returns the bottle to his breast pocket.*

CHASE  That should do it.

GRAY  If you don't see me anymore, I want you to have the TV.

CHASE  Okay.

GRAY  It's good to feel like you're a part of something.

GRAY *exits, closes the door.*

LYNCH  So you don't wanna be the elephant?

CHASE  Not right now.

LYNCH  You sure?

CHASE  Pretty sure, dude.

LYNCH  Okay.

LYNCH *crosses to the* BOY, *lifts him out of the chair, starts for the back of the apartment with him.*

ADAM RAPP

CHASE  Lynch.

LYNCH  Yeah?

CHASE  What are you gonna like do with, um, Pete?

LYNCH  I was gonna play him a song.

CHASE  Oh.

LYNCH  But first I'm gonna clean him. He's pretty dirty.

LYNCH *exits down the hall with the* BOY.

*Moments later, the window is opened.* STAPLES *climbs through with a large McDonald's bag in his mouth. He no longer wears his hat and his snowsuit has been partly blown off. He is bare-chested. There is ice in his hair and beard. He closes the window, turns to* CHASE.

STAPLES  (*as if caught in a blizzard*)
    *SNOW*
    *SNOW AND ICE*
    *SNOW AND ICE AND WIND*
    *SLEET IN THE TREES*
    *BIRDS FALLING TO THE PAVEMENT*
    *FROZEN PIGEONS ALL ACROSS TENTH STREET*
    *SO COLD THEY LOOK BLUE*
    *FROST CRAWLING UP THE SIDES OF BUILDINGS*
    *PEOPLE IN FRONT OF THEIR WINDOWS WEARING COATS*
    *SCARVES*
    *SKI MASKS*
    *THE MOON LOOKS LIKE A HUGE ICEBALL*

STAPLES *tosses* CHASE *his Happy Meal box, takes a seat on the stage-left end of the sofa, removes his own Happy Meal box, emptying the contents onto his lap.*

SPEED *enters from the back of the apartment wearing a welding mask, still in his underwear.* STAPLES *hands him his Happy Meal box.* CHASE *hands his to* SPEED *as well.* SPEED *thrusts the Happy Meal boxes into the air victoriously, then crosses to the Happy Meal wall, offers the new additions to the Happy Meal gods.*

CHASE *and* STAPLES *don't eat, but simply play with the toys contained inside.*

CHASE *uses the remote, finds his channel on the TV. Once again, the sound of the animal being tortured.* CHASE *and* STAPLES *are instantly mesmerized.*

LYNCH *enters from the back of the apartment in long underwear. He is no longer wearing the bear mask. There is a large knitting needle sticking out of his right foot. He is carrying* PETE, *who has been bathed and is now dressed in a "LESS: LESS IS MORE" T-shirt and a Burger King crown.*

CHASE *and* STAPLES *have fallen asleep.* LYNCH *watches the TV for a moment, then crosses to the sofa, places* PETE *between* CHASE *and* STAPLES, *limps over to the TV, places the vase of tulips on the coffee table, then rears back and kicks in* GRAY's *TV with his needled foot.* CHASE *and* STAPLES *continue sleeping.* SPEED *continues staring at the wall of Happy Meal boxes.*

LYNCH *crosses to the keyboard, taps on* SPEED's *welding mask. After no response he bends down, attempts to turns on the amp under the keyboard, fails, removes an electric guitar from under a heap of debris, plays unplugged while singing to the* BOY:

LYNCH (singing)

    *the element man*
    *collecting noble gases*
    *monatomic plan*
    *helium scam*
    *argon passes*

    *he's got a distance machine*
    *powered by rocket fuel*
    *he's got a color TV*
    *and some microwave tea*
    *to navigate his reprieve*

    *distance, area, and volume*
    *space so hard to find*

LYNCH *collapses, slowly gets to his feet. He crosses to the sofa, gathers the* BOY *in his arms. Lights fade to a rich blue out.*

Bottomside's *"40 Holes and 40 Goals" plays. During the song,* LYNCH *dances with the* BOY. *It's a childlike waltz. He turns a few slow circles throughout the apartment. The dance eventually leads to the hallway and then to the back of the apartment.* STAPLES *wakes, watches* LYNCH *make his way to the back of the apartment with the* BOY.

    *there's a hole*
    *in my head*
    *there's a hole*
    *in my pocket*
    *there's a hole*

in the floor
there's a hole
in the door
i'm gonna find it
i'm gonna fill it

The light grows very dark and strange on the window. After a moment
he rises off the sofa, finds an old, discarded T-shirt, puts it on, crosses to
the window, which is now completely covered with frost.

there's a hole
in my mattress
there's a hole
in my hand
there's a hole
in the afternoon
there's a hole
in the room
i'm gonna find it
i'm gonna fill it
there's a hole

STAPLES reaches out and touches the window. He withdraws his hand,
and crosses to GRAY's TV. He bends down and puts his hand through
the hole, retracts it, stares at his hand, turns to the bowl of pills. He
reaches in and takes a blue. Then another. Then another. Then several
more. He swallows them all. He takes a pink. Swallows. And then a
yellow. STAPLES swallows the pills, slowly and deliberately, staring out.

there's a hole
in the window

*there's a hole*
*in the wall*
*there's a hole*
*in my shower*
*there's a hole*
*in the hour*
*i'm gonna find it*
*i'm gonna fill it*
*with a flower*

STAPLES *returns to the sofa, removes a tulip from the vase, still standing, grabs it, regards it for a moment and then starts to eat the petals one by one while turning a slow circle.*

*After he has eaten all the petals, he sits in his spot on the sofa, leans back, staring out.*

*huh-huh-huh*
*huh-huh-huh . . .*

STAPLES *closes his eyes.*

*The blue light slowly changes to a strange pink light on* STAPLES.

*The song ends.*

*Lights fade to black.*

*Lights slowly fade up.*

*The apartment is filled with yellow light.*

*Finer Noble Gases*

*It is now morning.*

*As before, CHASE and STAPLES are asleep on the couch, STAPLES holding the stem of the eaten tulip.*

*SPEED is back on the floor, now asleep, still wearing the welding mask.*

*A cell phone rings four times, then ceases.*

*LYNCH enters from the back of the apartment. He wears his long underwear. The areas of his shins, arms, forehead, thighs, face, and hands are grotesquely bloody. There are several needles sticking out of his foot. He is carrying his brick. He is also holding the elephant mask.*

*A cell phone rings again.*

*LYNCH stops, turns toward the sound of the cell phone. He leans over CHASE, grabs his cell phone, answers it.*

LYNCH  Hello? . . . Lynch . . . Hey, Mr. Fitzsimmons . . . Yeah, he's here, but he's sleeping . . . Sure, I'll give him a message . . . Okay . . . Bye.

*LYNCH turns the phone off, places it next to CHASE. He stares at him a moment, then shakes him. CHASE stirs, wakes.*

CHASE  Hey, Lynch.
LYNCH  Hey. Your dad called.
CHASE  When?
LYNCH  Just now.

CHASE  Oh. What'd he want?

LYNCH  He said he heard about the storm.

CHASE  What storm.

LYNCH  The snowstorm. He just wanted to let you know he heard about it.

*A beat.*

CHASE  Dude, what happened?

LYNCH  What.

CHASE  You're all bloody.

LYNCH  I woke up in the middle of the night and this robot was hitting me with the brick . . . But I took care of him . . . There's metal everywhere back there . . .

*The brick falls to the floor.* LYNCH *slowly crosses to the window, looks out for a moment, then expires.*

GRAY *enters. He is wearing the same gray suit and tie and an odd-shaped bowler hat. He is wet with snow. He is holding a bloody knife. There's blood and vomit on the front of his suit. He is shivering.*

GRAY  Hi.

CHASE  Hey, Gray.

GRAY  Hi.

GRAY *stands very still.*

GRAY  It's really cold out. Lots of snow.

CHASE  You're holding a knife, dude.

GRAY  Yeah.

*Finer Noble Gases*                                                    235

CHASE  And there's like blood on it.

GRAY  When it goes in, it feels like nothing. It's so light. Even. Like nowhere. You think there will be screaming. Fighting. Music in the background. Like on TV. But it's not like that. Not if you put it in the way they show you. In the part where the voice makes a noise. It was so quiet. And he just sat down. He just sat down like he was old and tired. Like he'd walked for a long time and needed to rest . . .

It's so good to feel like you're a part of something.

*GRAY crosses to the tulips, gathers them in his arms.*

GRAY  My lamp broke. I knocked it over when I unplugged the TV. Broke into a thousand pieces. It's really cold down there. (*he starts to weep*) Can I stay up here with you? I'll be really still. Just a few days.

CHASE  Sure, Gray, sure.

GRAY  I won't move, hardly at all.

CHASE  No problem buddy.

GRAY  I heard the Sun's coming.

*GRAY slowly crosses to the beer sign, steps onto the chair, turns it on. His movements are very slow, as though he is coming to some kind of expiration. He turns the sign on and starts to arrange the tulips in the light over the following:*

CHASE  (*to* GRAY) I had this dream last night . . . I was a robot . . . Big metal robot . . . I was crying but nothing was coming out . . . No tears . . . And I didn't have any balls . . . Instead I had a light switch . . . I kept trying to turn it on but all it did was make this buzzing noise . . .

CHASE *plants his feet on the floor for the first time, slowly stands, takes in the room for a moment.*

CHASE *(to* GRAY*)* I . . . I can't feel my feet.

STAPLES*'s cell phone starts to ring.* CHASE *thinks it's his. He checks. It's not. He turns to* STAPLES *at the other end of the sofa.*

*The cell phone rings again.*

CHASE *reaches over, shakes him.* STAPLES *doesn't stir.*

CHASE *touches his cheek, draws his hand back, quickly retreats to his side of the sofa.*

GRAY *continues to stare at the tulips arranged in the beer light.*

SPEED *slowly begins to rise off the floor.*

CHASE *starts to weep.*

*Blackout as the cell phone rings through the silence.*

*Lights up.*

*The apartment is still dark but a soft yellow light is starting to come through the window.* CHASE *is holding an electric guitar, ready to play.* STAPLES *is at one of the microphone stands, upright, very much alive.* SPEED *is seated at the drum set, no longer wearing the welding mask.* LYNCH *is facing the drums, strapped with the bass.* STAPLES *starts to sing "The Astronaut's Lament." It starts slowly*

*Finer Noble Gases*

and then builds into an up-beat pop song, then opens up into aggressive
punk rock.

STAPLES  (singing)
  in the very tiny hours
  when the night turns into the day
  when your spaceships come
  and steal your plans
  and make your blue skies change to gray

  i sit alone in my room
  how can i be so lazy
  when the astronauts are giving it one more try
  why does the stratosphere look so hazy?

All the lights come on. It should be very bright in the theater now.

  22 days ago
  i saw a number cruncher lookin at me
  he had a bowling ball tied to his bum left leg
  and he walked into the sea

  and he went down, down, down, down
  down to the end of the pier

  he jumped and drowned, drowned, drowned, drowned
  but he couldn't get there from here

  the junk dealer's getting his fix
  the radio ain't playing songs

ADAM RAPP

the kid downstairs is wearing my 3-piece suit
should I make my body strong?

the chief of police lost his gun
the subway map is missing a stop
the rifle dealer's taking a cigarette break
i wonder what he's got in stock?

my corduroy pants are too small
i think my dog is runnin away
if the eskimos can build a house outta snow
then maybe I can build one with hay

and he went down, down, down, down
down to the end of the pier

he jumped and drowned, drowned, drowned, drowned
but he couldn't get there from here

The song slows down suddenly. A "freak-out."

SPEED is excellent at the drums.

CHASE is superior on the guitar.

LYNCH grooves with the bass.

STAPLES turns on the keyboard during the instrumental break.

*The whole of it turns into an extended jam session with inspired improvisation. After a minute or so, they find the bass line and return to the chorus.*

> *and he went down, down, down, down*
> *down to the end of the pier*
>
> *he jumped and drowned, drowned, drowned, drowned*
> *but he couldn't get there from here*
>
> *and he went down, down, down, down*
> *down to the end of the pier*
> *he jumped and drowned, drowned, drowned, drowned*
> *but he couldn't get there from here*

*On the final run of the drums, before the crash of the symbols, the band freezes in a strobe of white light.*

ADAM RAPP